Pilgrimage as Rite of P

A Guidebook
for
Youth Ministry

by

Robert J. Brancatelli

PAULIST PRESS
New York/Mahwah, N.J.

For Rita Claire Dorner and Anne Marie Mongoven:
teachers, catechists, friends

Cover photograph and interior photographs by W.P. Wittman, Ltd., Toronto.

Cover design by Vitale Communications

Library of Congress Cataloging-in-Publication Data

Brancatelli, Robert J.,   1956–
    Pilgrimage as rite of passage : a guidebook for youth ministry / by Robert J. Brancatelli.
        p.   cm.
    Includes bibliographical references.
    ISBN 0-8091-3798-4 (alk. paper)
    1. Church work with youth—Catholic Church. 2. Christian pilgrims and pilgrimages. 3. Catholic Church—Education. I. Title.
BX2347.8.Y7B73   1998
259'.23—dc21
                                                                                    98–10840
                                                                                    CIP

Published by Paulist Press
997 Macarthur Boulevard
Mahwah, New Jersey 07430

Printed and bound in the
United States of America

Contents

INTRODUCTION

The first question you may ask in picking up this book is, why a pilgrimage? Doesn't that have to do with Lourdes, Fatima, Medjugorje and the Crusades? How is pilgrimage a rite of passage, and why would adolescents—teenagers—on the brink of the twenty-first century be interested in something so arcane?

Well, I'm not sure myself. But I know they are, and I have seen proof of this on pilgrimages to Denver, Colorado and Manila, the Philippines for World Youth Day. During those events, youth from the ages of twelve to twenty responded to Pope John Paul II's call to celebrate their Christian faith together and "take up the challenge of making Christ known in the modern metropolis." I witnessed hearts softened and lives changed by these experiences. And it wasn't just travel that affected these youth, although traveling halfway around the world with thousands of other youth is certainly a mysterious and thrilling (and loud) experience.

But there was something more, something that touched many "pilgrims" and inspired them to make the faith their own, or at least begin the process. These experiences with World Youth Day inspired me to study pilgrimage as a model for conversion, and to ask some questions about what made it such a life-changing experience for so many youth. What was confirmed in subsequent pilot programs with both younger and older teens is that the "test" is a big part of the process. Youth feel better about themselves for having made it through the trials and discomforts of a pilgrimage experience. When this occurs in a faith context, the results are impressive. Youth make the connections between their own "culture" and the Christian faith that others—family, friends, pastors, DREs—have tried so hard to pass on. I have seen this happen again and again both in my work in youth ministry in California and elsewhere.

Pilgrimage as Rite of Passage is the result of this experience. It is a process whereby youth can test their limits and discover their potential as individuals and members of the church community. These are the two dimensions of adolescent conversion the process hinges on: (1) a test or trial of one's ability and gifts and (2) the affirmation that comes from living and working together in a community. *Pilgrimage as Rite of Passage* has been tested "on the road" in California at the diocesan and parish levels as a rite of passage and as part of a confirmation program for older teens. I have witnessed many youth begin the rite as adolescents and end it with a clearer vision of what it means to be an *adult* Christian. For that reason, the rite is not

1

meant to be easy. It is not a pious formality or feel-good ritual. Nor is it confirmation. It is designed to acknowledge and celebrate the often tough transition to adulthood, and youth have to work every step of the way to make it happen.

Since many dioceses throughout the country are looking at restoring the sequence of the sacraments of initiation—baptism, confirmation, Eucharist—a rite of passage for adolescents can fill the void during the teenage years. *Pilgrimage as Rite of Passage* can be used in just such instances, thereby restoring confirmation to its proper place in initiation and meeting the pastoral needs of adolescents, their families and the parish community. But, like confirmation, this rite is not a "graduation." It is meant to encourage greater participation among youth in the worship and faith life of the church. In doing so, it has become an effective method of evangelization and catechesis.

This rite may be done in English, Spanish, Vietnamese or other languages. It may also be combined with on-going ethnic rituals such as Mexican *quince años* celebrations. It can be adapted as part of a confirmation program or used with the RCIA and existing ministry programs. Hopefully, it will inspire participants to become more involved with their church community and deepen their faith. Over the long term, it can renew and invigorate the entire community.

THE RITE

With this as background, I need to make several comments about the particulars of the rite. First, there's a lot going on. The rite contains one introductory meeting, three catechetical sessions, a prepilgrimage ritual (Circle Dance), the pilgrimage and a mystagogia session. That doesn't include interviews with prospective pilgrims, planning and evaluation meetings and any commissioning or welcoming ceremonies the catechist or team may want to create. Obviously, doing the rite in its entirety is a big commitment of time, resources, people and energy. It's certainly worth it, but doing just parts (the catechetical sessions, for example) or incorporating prayers into pre-existing programs (confirmation) has proven helpful for some parishes and schools.

Second, the catechetical sessions are heavily biblical. They present youth with biblical texts they may not be familiar with and offer a fresh understanding of the role of scripture in the church's faith. Youth may also find that the Bible isn't as boring and irrelevant as they may have thought.[1] Of course, the catechist and team can substitute liturgical, dogmatic or social justice themes for the shared faith reflection in place of scripture. This may be appropriate if the rite coincides with a major liturgical feast or season. Participants will still hear scripture readings during the ritual prayers for each catechetical session.

Third, prayer is an important element in the rite. Each catechetical session opens and closes with ritual prayer, so youth will get the idea that everything that occurs between these ritual prayers *is* prayer. Consideration of the human experience, discussion, dialogue, sharing and ritual acts are all part of the prayer. Real life is prayer. Prayer is not something done only at mealtime. Youth may also discover that Christ is present in their personal and collective experiences and that those experiences must be brought into the community's worship.

2

And last, since this rite involves outdoor activities, summer may be a better time to conduct the pilgrimage. It could easily fit into a summer youth ministry program. If the rite is performed at a school without a summer schedule, Lent would be a good alternative both weather-wise and liturgically. In either case, the catechist and team should make a clear distinction between this rite and confirmation. In those dioceses with middle school or high school confirmation programs, the team should think seriously about the placement of the rite—*before* confirmation is better. Again, some parishes/schools have adapted parts of the rite in their confirmation programs.

WHAT'S INSIDE?

This book is divided into three chapters. Chapter 1 contains the catechetical sessions. Chapter 2 presents the pilgrimage, Circle Dance and a mystagogia session. Chapter 3 is a "Reflection on the Rite," which provides background and research on adolescents and pilgrimage. In Chapter 1, the presumption is that the catechist knows the youth and is willing to perform the entire process (from organization of the team and initial interviews through all three sessions). Also, since the rite relies heavily on supplemental material, the catechist should prepare by referencing the catechist resources on page 62. The material on vision quest, journaling, fasting and the medicine walk is extremely important.

Chapter 2 presents the Circle Dance (a prepilgrimage ritual involving males and females), the pilgrimage and a mystagogia session. The dance and mystagogia session offer a detailed process to follow. However, the pilgrimage gives only an outline for planning, objectives, site selection, agenda and equipment list. The catechist/team make the specific arrangements for the event, keeping in mind the purpose and goals of the process and adapting it to meet the actual needs of the youth. The mystagogia session resumes the catechetical format of Chapter 1.

Chapter 3 analyzes the psychological development of youth according to Erik Erikson's theory of identity-formation. According to Erikson, the major task of adolescence is the formation of an identity and sense of belonging. This sense of belonging may be to another person, group, community or ideal. Working with this model, Carol Gilligan of Harvard University later discovered differences among males and females that can have a direct bearing on the use of pilgrimage as a rite of passage. Therefore, the three catechetical sessions deal with males and females separately (see Chapter 3).

The third chapter also examines the need for ritual among youth and then closes with a model of catechesis developed by Anne Marie Mongoven of Santa Clara University. This model includes a detailed process for working with groups, a shared reflection on a faith theme and ritual prayer. The process is needs-based and community-oriented. Additionally, all catechetical sessions in the rite are divided by gender to help youth develop a greater sense of group identity and belonging.

Finally, *Pilgrimage as Rite of Passage* should be viewed as a *suggestion* for ways to involve youth in the church. It is not filled with rules about what to do or not to do. It presumes creativity and energy on the part of the catechist/team. This may be especially important in the area of sexuality, which is an important part of identity-formation. Youth are particularly aware of their sexual drive and may have questions about their own sexuality and gender roles. This is a normal and healthy part of identity. They should be warned that sexual images, fantasies and the like may appear during fasting, hiking, sitting up for the vigil and at other times during the rite. This is another reason for separation by gender. The adult team can do tremendous good by being present and available for pilgrims when they have questions or problems.

CHAPTER ONE

BACKGROUND

Pilgrimage as Rite of Passage consists of four parts. The first part presents catechetical sessions dealing with the challenges youth face, their gifts for meeting these challenges and the creation of a group identity. Each of these, in turn, corresponds to the three stages of passage: *separation, liminality* and *reintegration.* The second part involves journaling; fasting, which youth do on their own under the supervision of the leadership team; and a medicine walk. The third part is the Circle Dance and pilgrimage, which entails a day-long trip to a remote site, a lengthy hike and fasting. The final part is the mystagogia session, during which pilgrims reflect on their experience and commit themselves to volunteer work in parish ministry, community service, extracurricular activities at school and prayer.

This chapter contains three catechetical sessions lasting two hours each on *challenges, gifts* and *belonging.* All sessions follow Mongoven's process of catechesis and do not focus on any specific ethnic, cultural or geographic group. Rather, they present *guidelines* for the catechist and team as well as suggestions for adapting the readings and prayers for males/females. In some cases, the catechist may need to rework the sections on consideration of the human experience and shared faith reflection. The catechist should refer to the resource list for specific needs and program descriptions.

By all outward appearances, the pilgrimage and the preparation for it form the heart of the rite. Pilgrims prepare themselves by journaling, fasting, walking and participating in sessions. Some youth may come to view the pilgrimage as the entire rite, assuming they will "feel different" upon their return. This may be true, but the catechetical sessions are where they actually cross the threshold into adulthood. During these sessions they do more than prepare for the pilgrimage. They come face-to-face with their fears and discover their own ways of dealing with them. Ideally, by the last session they will have identified their greatest gift and how they can use it for the benefit of others. The pilgrimage tests and challenges their newfound identity, *confirming* what they discovered through the catechetical process.

Obviously, this rite may not work for everyone. Some may not get anything substantial out of the catechesis; others may look at the pilgrimage as just another field trip. Research shows that young women may not relate to the need for testing themselves, since their development centers primarily on bonding and forming relationships. The leadership team should adapt the rite to the specific needs of the youth, taking into account gender, language, culture and the psychological makeup of the group. Team members (men for males; women for females) should be available to talk to youth and guide them through the rite. Their chief role is that of mentor. Each team member is responsible for an assigned group of young men or young women. Team members also help youth with journaling, fasting and the medicine walk between sessions.

Journaling: Once the catechist has met with youth in an initial interview, he or she schedules a meeting prior to the first catechetical session to go over the rite and calendar, answer questions from youth and parents and distribute journals. *Youth begin writing in their journals every day and should be strongly encouraged to continue writing throughout the rite.* For example, in the first catechetical session youth write about their personal challenges, observing the ways they are affected by them. They also probe the possible causes and motives behind them. This will help them learn more about who they are and their limitations. The catechist or team can provide questions for youth to answer such as: "Who am I?" "What do I fear?" "Why must I die?" "What are my blessings?" "Who are my people?" "Who is Jesus?" "Where do I find Jesus?" "Who are my teachers?"

The youth will also want to use these journals as yearbooks, asking other youth to sign them and keeping them as mementos of the rite (see the *Mystagogia Session).*

Fasting: This is an ancient practice used with meditation and prayer. Youth abstain from eating for at least twelve hours to cleanse their bodies, sharpen their senses and discipline their minds. It will also prepare them for the twenty-four-hour fast on the pilgrimage. Youth should journal during the fast and meditate on Is 58:1–9(a). The fast should be planned with a team member and done some-time *prior to the second catechetical session.*

Note: *The team should be prepared for problems involving dieting, weight loss, anorexia and bulimia. These are often rooted in self-esteem issues and should be treated with extreme care. The catechist should have access to professional help and/or resources if an emergency develops. See* **Catechist Resources** *for suggested reading.*

Medicine Walk: This is a three-hour, *aimless* walk in a natural setting: forest, park, mountain, beach, country road, etc. Its purpose is to get youth in touch with the unconscious self by being unencumbered by tasks, work, school or other concerns. Therefore, journaling is an important part of the activity and should be done on the walk. There is no eating or snacking during the walk, which each youth does *alone.* Dawn or early morning is recommended. Youth need to come back from the walk with a meaningful symbol of their experience (rock, coin, can, feather, leaf, flower), which will be used in the third catechetical session. The medicine walk should be planned with an adult team member and done *prior to the third catechetical session.*[2]

Purpose of Gathering: All sessions are designed to prepare youth for their new role as adult members of the Christian community. They do this by relating the human experiences of challenge, gift and belonging to an overnight pilgrimage.

The catechetical sessions presented here require youth to perform journaling, fasting and a "medicine walk."[3]

Time, Place and Frequency: Suggested frequency for catechetical sessions is once a week for three consecutive weeks. Sessions should last no more than two hours. Since "all mysteries are celebrated at night," sessions should be held after sundown.[4] Youth perform journaling daily, a twelve-hour fast after the first catechetical session, a medicine walk after the second and a Circle Dance after the third. Also, the group meets prior to the program to review the rite and calendar, answer questions and distribute journals.

Total number of meetings:

- 1 introductory meeting
- 3 catechetical sessions
- 1 Circle Dance (pre-pilgrimage ritual)
- 1 pilgrimage
- 1 mystagogia session

Note: *The catechist should consider holding a training session for the team, covering such topics as adolescent development, ritual, pilgrimage, group facilitation, counseling, etc. See* **Catechist Resources** *for suggested materials.*

Environment: Unless indicated otherwise, sessions are held informally either in a parish or high school lounge, meeting room or home. Participants should have ample space and not feel cramped. The environment needs to be intimate, prayerful and non-threatening. Also, the use of color is important. Whenever possible, *red* decor should be used for the sessions with males; *yellow* with females. The leadership team will distribute colored bandannas during the Circle Dance.

Profile of Participants:

Age and gender

Recommended ages are 14 to 18, although the catechist should determine this with youth/parents/teachers. Process involves separating males and females for all three catechetical sessions. However, the Circle Dance, pilgrimage and mystagogia session are done jointly.

Cultural makeup

It is best to have a culturally, ethnically and linguistically diverse group. This provides a learning and sharing environment for youth and reinforces the value of catholicity in the church. The catechist/team should make sure that resource material, music and liturgies reflect the group's multicultural makeup.

Education

There is no educational requirement, but youth should have sufficient faith formation to benefit from the sessions and pilgrimage. The rite of passage may be made available to all youth (including non-Catholics) with follow-up with the RCIA, *only if appropriate.*

Participation in the parish/school

Please, no minimum requirements or service hours! However, youth should be strongly encouraged to seek volunteer opportunities that best match their gifts,

talents and willingness to serve *after* the rite. This can be done as part of the mystagogia session (see *Mystagogia Session,* "Acting Justly").

Motivation

The catechist interviews all prospective youth, identifying their motives and reasons for participating. Youth need to understand the commitment they are making to the entire rite (sessions, Circle Dance, pilgrimage, etc.). Beyond a sincere desire to participate in the rite, youth should not have to go through "hoops" to qualify. There are no minimum qualifications or restrictions. This rite should be made available to everyone of age.

SESSION ONE: CHALLENGES

1. LIFE SIGN:

Youth making the transition to adulthood experience tremendous pressure psychologically, emotionally, spiritually and physically. The source of this pressure lies in their need for an identity related to and yet distinct from their parents and family. This rite, therefore, treats the human experiences of *challenge, gift* and *belonging* as they are experienced in the lives of young people. Each of the three catechetical sessions will cover one of these experiences. Session one begins with the human experience of "challenge." What are the challenges young people face at home, school, work? How do these challenges affect them? How do they respond?

2. TIME, PLACE AND FREQUENCY:
(see page 7 of BACKGROUND, chapter one.)

3. ENVIRONMENT:
(see page 7 of BACKGROUND, chapter one.)

4. PROFILE OF PARTICIPANTS:
(see pages 7–8 of BACKGROUND, chapter one.)

5. BIBLICAL SIGN:

Males

The parable of the Prodigal Son (Lk 15:11–32) will be used as the biblical sign for the shared faith reflection. Discussion of the parable should include the challenges the younger son faced at home as well as on the road and his reasons for returning to his father's house. The catechist should relate the parable to issues raised during consideration of the human experience. This parable contains the three stages of initiation: separation (11–16), liminal period (17–20a) and reintegration into the community (20b–24). The reaction of the older son (25–32) is also important to the overall process of initiation and should be included. Many adolescents may identify with it readily.

Females

The story of Suzanna and the Elders (Dn 13:1–64) is the biblical sign for the shared faith reflection. Discussion should include the challenges Suzanna faces with the two elders, her family and the faith community. As a morality play, this story lends itself to role playing, which may be used in place of the activity for the human experience. If the catechist chooses to do this, the story is first read to the group and then the principal parts (Suzanna, the elders, Daniel, the crowd) acted out. The catechist should allow enough time for reactions to the role playing as well as group analysis. The role playing may be done in place of both consideration of the human experience and the shared faith reflection. After role playing, the catechist moves directly to acting justly. (Suggested text is Dn 13:1–9, 12, 15–52[a], 54, 56, 58, 60–62.)

The liberation songs of women prophets may be used as alternatives to Suzanna and the Elders. These include the Song of Miriam (Ex 15:20–21), the Song of Deborah (Jgs 4,5), Judith (Jdt 16) and the Magnificat of Mary (Lk 1:46–55). Ruth and Esther also provide good reflection material for the challenges young women face. In selecting a biblical sign, the leadership team should look at how well the story relates to young women rather than its adherence to initiation theory. A liturgical or ecclesial sign may prove useful, including appropriate material from *quince años* celebrations in either English or Spanish. For an excellent treatment of women in the Hebrew scriptures, see Miriam Therese Winter,

Woman Witness: A Feminist Lectionary and Psalter, Women of the Hebrew Scriptures: Part Two (New York: Crossroad, 1992). Winter offers points for shared reflection, prayers and "psalms" for a number of women "witnesses."

In addition, the Book of Job offers numerous passages suitable for a catechetical session on challenges for both males and females. The classic story of conversion follows the stages of separation (1–3:2), liminality (3:3–40:5) and reintegration (40:6–42:17).

6. OBJECTIVES:

The objectives of the first session on challenges are:

(1)   to create community among youth,

(2)   to urge youth to name and then share the challenges they face,

(3)   to relate scripture to these challenges,

(4)   to motivate youth to respond to their challenges collectively,

(5)   to experience the spirituality of gender through ritual prayer.

7. CATECHIST REFLECTION: See BACKGROUND.

8. PROCESS OF CATECHESIS:

(1) Welcoming   10 minutes
Youth assemble outside the room where the session will be held. The adult team leads them in procession with the Easter candle into the room. This is done in silence. Before entering, all youth remove their shoes. Then the catechist or other team member pours cold water over their hands from a baptismal font or large basin, reciting Ez 36:25–26: "I will pour clean water on you and I will give you a new heart, a new spirit within you, says the Lord" (*The Rites of the Catholic Church,* vol. 1, "Rite of Confirmation," 58. Pueblo: The Liturgical Press, 1990). The youth enter and take their places on the floor around the prayer center. Adults remain standing.

The prayer center should be a focal point containing either a cross, large candle, incense burner, Bible, chalice, icon, image of *Nuestra Señora de Guadalupe* or other meaningful Christian symbol. After everyone has gathered, the door should be closed to prevent distraction and heighten the sense of separation from the outside world. This is done for both males and females.

Note: *Since this is a ritual welcome, ice-breakers or other community-building activities should be planned before this first session. A good time to do these activities would be during the introductory meeting. The catechist/team should plan these activities carefully since youth need to feel comfortable with each other and the team in order to participate fully in the catechetical process. The catechist may choose to hold one or two additional meetings before the sessions begin.*

(2) Gathering prayer
After a period of silence the prayer leader asks the youth to stand and says the following prayer adapted from the rite of confirmation:

All-loving God,
with water and the Holy Spirit
you freed your sons (daughters) from death
and gave them new life.

Send your Holy Spirit upon them now
as they face the challenges

and uncertainties of man(woman)hood.
We ask this through Christ our brother.
R. Amen.

(The "Rite of Confirmation")

(3) Human experience to be considered: challenges   35 minutes

After the prayer the youth sit in a circle around the prayer center. The catechist introduces the topic of "challenges in life" and asks the youth to think seriously about the greatest challenge they face. Then the catechist asks them to write a brief description of the challenge in their journals (see **Journaling**). The catechist pairs off the group, allowing time for sharing. Team members offer help in identifying challenges. The catechist then calls the group together and leads a discussion with the following or similar questions:

What makes something a challenge?
What are some of the challenges you face as young men/young women? Why?
Did you find any similarity between your challenge and your partner's?
Is your challenge self-imposed, or does it come from other people such as family, friends, teachers?
How do you respond to your challenge?
Do you look for help, or do you go it alone?
How does your challenge make you feel?
Do you consider your challenge permanent or merely temporary? Why?
As you get older, do the challenges become harder or easier?

At the end of this time, the catechist summarizes the challenges the youth identified, relating them to the following faith story.

(4) Shared faith reflection   25 minutes

Males

The catechist uses the parable of the Prodigal Son (Lk 15:11–32) for the shared faith reflection. The catechist may introduce the reading by asking youth to listen for similarities between the parable and their own experiences. The catechist can also ask them to put themselves in the role of the younger son. After reading the parable slowly, the catechist pauses for a moment and asks the following or similar questions:

> What are the challenges the younger son faces at home?
> Why does he leave home?
> Why does the father allow him to leave?
> What are the challenges the younger son faces on the road?
> Why does he return home?
> Why does the father welcome him back?
> What do you suppose the son has learned?
> Would he have learned it if he had stayed at home?
> What has the father learned?
> What do you think of the older son's reaction?
> What does this parable say about your own experience?

It is important for the catechist to relate the story to participants' experience. This may be done by discussing the story in terms of the comments made during consideration of the human experience. Also, the catechist should emphasize the need of the younger son *to leave* his physical surroundings in order to achieve a deeper spiritual understanding of himself. The catechist can connect this to the role of pilgrimage in finding one's true identity.

Females

The same process is followed with young women. Again, the catechist should emphasize the challenges Suzanna faces and how she overcomes them (Dn 13:1–64). The catechist asks the following or similar questions:

> What are the challenges Suzanna faces?
> How does she overcome them?
> Why does the community believe the elders?
> How does her family react?
> What does Suzanna ask of God?
> How would you have reacted in the garden?
> Would you pray for God's help or try to deal with the
>   situation yourself?
> Have you had a similar experience?
> How did you deal with it?
> What does this story say about the challenges girls and
>   women face in society?
> Could this have happened to a young man?

(5) Acting justly   20 minutes

The catechist forms small groups (4–5 per group) and asks each group to think of ways to respond *collectively* to the needs surfaced in the session. This will give youth a sense of community as pilgrims and remind them of their social responsibility as Christians. Then each group reports briefly to the large group. The catechist

and youth may decide to implement the group responses at a later time as part of the rite. If so, the catechist/team should make the necessary adjustments to the calendar.

(6) Closing prayer   15 minutes

Different closing prayers are used for the young men and women. However, the purpose of both prayers is twofold: to deepen gender identity among group members and create a spirituality based on that identity.

Males

Gathering activity: The gathering activity is drumming. The drumming should be soft and rhythmic, marking a clear distinction between what went before and what follows. The young men stand in a tight circle around the prayer center, which contains incense and a candle (or candles). The prayer leader leads everyone in a simple chant such as the Jesus Prayer or similar intonation.

Reading: Abruptly, the chanting and drumming stop. A team member lights the candle(s) in the prayer center, and the leader reads a portion of the passage used in the shared faith reflection. Example: Lk 15:11–6 (separation).

Leader: "The Gospel of the Lord."
     R.   "Praise to you, Lord Jesus Christ."

Response to reading: After a brief period of silence, the young men strip to the waist for the signing of the senses. Depending on the number of youth, the prayer leader may do the signing himself or involve other team members. Perfumed oil is used for the signing, which is done on the forehead, lips and above the heart.

Leader: Receive the sign of the cross on your forehead,
              that you may remember your Lord.

Receive the sign of the cross on your lips,
that you may say yes to the Word of God.

Receive the sign of the cross on your heart,
that Jesus may dwell there forever.

R. Amen.[5]

Petitions: Petitions may be made by anyone in the group. The leader begins:

Leader: "Loving God, we ask you for the courage to bear our challenges as your Son bore the cross. For this we pray."
    R.   "Lord, hear our prayer."

Our Father: Everyone prays standing in a close circle and holding hands.

Ritual action: The catechist/prayer leader presents a wooden cross or appropriate symbol of brotherhood to each candidate.

Closing song: Drumming may be done again but in a different, faster and more lively tempo. The music, if sung, should be within a suitable range for young men and relate to the theme of challenges.

Females

Gathering activity: The same gathering activity with drumming and chanting may be used. The leadership team may include guitar, violin, piano or flute music. Wooden flute music and group movement offer creative alternatives for gathering young women. Although this session corresponds to the separation stage of the rite, the activity should bring the young women closer together. A physical activity like group dance or movement is ideal.[6]

Reading: Suggested text for the prayer is Dn 13:42–44.

Response to reading: The response to the reading should involve a group activity that reinforces sisterhood and community. Examples include singing, chanting, dancing, anointing with water or oil, "smudging" with smoke, sharing food or engaging in activities with paint, sand or textiles. *Adult leaders should participate in the ritual as much as possible.*

Petitions: Petitions are directed toward Mary, asking her to pray for and intercede on behalf of the candidates.

      R.   "Mary, our sister, pray for us."

Our Father: Everyone prays standing in a close circle and holding hands.

Ritual action: As in the closing prayer for young men, the leadership team presents them with a wooden cross or other symbol of their bond to each other and to Christ. If possible, the symbol should express female images of faith and God.

Closing song: Similar to gathering activity.

9. PARTICIPANTS' RESOURCES:

The catechist/team supplies journals, pens, paper, crosses, prayer center items, musical instruments and music, art supplies, bandannas and other material for the catechetical and mystagogia sessions and liturgies. Youth are responsible for fasting and the medicine walk, which means they must have hiking shoes, appropriate clothing, juices and other liquids. Also, they must obtain their own supplies for the hike and overnight pilgrimage. See the pilgrimage section for a full equipment list.

10. EVALUATION:

The leadership team fills out the following evaluation. They should try to meet immediately after the session, but if this is not possible, the catechist should schedule a time *prior* to the next session for evaluation.

Please rate how well the catechetical session on challenges met the following objectives for youth, (1) low (4) high:

(1)	Created a sense of community	1	2	3	4
(2)	Urged naming and sharing of challenges	1	2	3	4
(3)	Related scripture to challenges	1	2	3	4
(4)	Formed a group response to challenges	1	2	3	4
(5)	Strengthened group identity through ritual prayer	1	2	3	4

- What was the best part of the session?
- What needs to be improved?
- How prepared was the team in organizing/leading the session?
- Was the team present and helpful to youth? Why/why not?
- What changes should be made for the next session?
  Comments/Suggestions:

Youth fill out the second evaluation.

Please rate how well tonight's catechetical session on challenges did in the following areas, (1) low (4) high:

(1)	Created a sense of community	1	2	3	4
(2)	Urged naming and sharing of challenges	1	2	3	4
(3)	Related scripture to challenges	1	2	3	4
(4)	Formed a group response to challenges	1	2	3	4
(5)	Strengthened group identity through ritual prayer	1	2	3	4

- What, if anything, surprised you about tonight's session?
- What did you like best?
- What would you change/add/delete?
  Comments/Suggestions:

11. MOTIVATIONAL TECHNIQUES:

The best motivational technique is relying on the witness of other youth and young adults who have "made their pilgrimage" and want to share their experience with others. This group may be highly motivated and serve as a source of potential members for leadership teams in the future. Also, parishes and schools may want to emphasize the "non-official" nature of the rite. Youth will respond best to programs that are creative, bold, different and offer some meaning in their lives. Parents, too, may welcome the rite as a help with their own struggles raising teenagers. They will be gratified to learn that the faith story and church play as central a role as in any high school confirmation program.

Another simple but highly effective technique is food. At the end of each catechetical session, the team should provide a social for youth, their parents and team members that includes snacks, drinks, coffee, tea and food prepared by the parish community. It would be helpful to have different ethnic food representing the community. This will give youth more time for community-building and connecting with adult mentors.

Again, community-building must not be left to chance. The catechist/team should plan activities with the specific needs of the group in mind. It is important to encourage youth to participate in the process without coercing them or making them feel uncomfortable. It is also important to monitor cliques and other potential problems. See **Catechist Resources,** especially Robert Bolton: *People Skills: How to Assert Yourself, Listen to Others and Resolve Conflicts.*

SESSION TWO: GIFTS

1. PURPOSE OF GATHERING:

The second catechetical session helps youth discover a gift or talent for overcoming the challenges faced in session one. This gift is their primary one: the one that defines who they are and the direction they should take in life (relationships, school, career). During the pilgrimage, they will choose a name for themselves that is related in some way to the gift discovered in this session.

2–4. These items remain the same. There is no change in time, environment or profile of candidates. Refer to BACKGROUND of chapter one for details.

5. LIFE SIGN:

There is a great deal of confusion among young people about who they are and where they belong. As seen in chapter one, youth need to discover what they are good at, their limitations and how others perceive them. They also need to begin making choices about career, work, school and relationships. Session two continues the theme of identity by helping youth identify their unique gifts. These gifts will help them overcome the challenges they face and build their self-confidence.

6. BIBLICAL SIGN:

Males

Jeremiah's call and commission (Jer 1:4–10) will be used as the biblical sign for the shared faith reflection. In this reading God confirms Jeremiah as a prophet to all the nations and blesses him by touching his lips and putting holy words in his mouth. At first Jeremiah thinks himself unworthy because he is "only a boy" who does not know "how to speak," but God admonishes him for thinking so lowly of himself and tells him he will be a prophet to all people. God encourages Jeremiah by assuring him, "I am with you to deliver you."

This reading is a perfect example of discerning one's gifts by listening to and being open to God's call. Sometimes the gift or talent is not obvious, or it may appear to be completely out of character with the individual. However, individual gifts must not be judged simply on a personal level. God called Jeremiah for the benefit of the Hebrew people so that they might repent of idolatry and unjust living. Jeremiah was God's instrument in the salvation of the entire community. God's call may come to anyone at any time, including adolescents struggling to find their own place and purpose in life.

Females

The reading for females is the Annunciation story (Lk 1:26–38), in which Mary accepts God's will for her and becomes a "servant of the Lord." She arrives at her gifts of inspiration and insight through personal struggle and reflection. This is similar to and yet different from Jeremiah's experience. The Annunciation is an excellent example of how young women can discern their gifts by being open to God's call and persevering in their response to that call.

7. OBJECTIVES:

The objectives of the second session on gifts are:

(1)   to continue building community among youth,

(2)   to help youth discover their unique gifts through stories and sharing,

(3)   to learn how giftedness is discovered and shared in scripture,

(4)   to form a group commitment for using gifts,

(5)   to express giftedness in ritual prayer.

8. CATECHIST REFLECTION:

The purpose of this session is to help youth answer the question, "Who am I?" They do this by identifying *one* gift they have been given by God that makes them unique. This will challenge them to think critically and build their self-confidence. The catechist and leadership team should encourage youth to discern gifts that may not be readily apparent (the scripture readings will help). Of course, they will not finish the process in one session, but they should at least *start* the self-reflection necessary at this liminal stage in the rite. Hopefully, their fasting prior to this session will stimulate reflection and group discussion.

The variety of gifts that exist in a group may include physical beauty, athletic prowess, sensitivity, humor, kindness, compassion, intellectual and artistic ability, wit, honesty, sincerity, optimism, mechanical inventiveness, devotion, loyalty, responsibility, perseverance, strength and leadership qualities. Even the ability to recognize giftedness in others is a gift (e.g., the composer Antonio Salieri's recognizing Mozart's giftedness in the 1985 movie *Amadeus*). These gifts are traits or characteristics that distinguish one individual from another.

Regarding giftedness and gender, it is important for the catechist to understand that the identity-formation process is different for males and females. As noted in chapter three, males struggle with separation issues in which they attempt to declare a certain degree of independence from family and authority figures. Females, however, are more apt to form friendships, growing through community and reliance on others rather than separation. Also, this process may be different yet again for Asian, Latino and African-American youth. Giftedness, therefore, does not necessarily imply *isolation* or distinction from the group or community.

9. PROCESS OF CATECHESIS:

(1) Welcoming   10 minutes

As in the first session, youth assemble outside the meeting room and remove their shoes. The adult team leads them in a procession with the Easter candle. The person bearing the candle places it in the prayer center as the catechist burns incense. This action should be accompanied by drumming, chanting or singing (songs may be taken from parish/school resources or **Catechist Resources**).

(2) Gathering prayer

As the youth gather in a circle, the prayer leader says the following prayer adapted from the rite of confirmation:

Gift-giving God,
you gave us the greatest gift
in Jesus, your only son and our brother.

Strengthen us now so we may find
gifts deep within us,
and touch us as you touched Jeremiah
(as Mary did when she said yes to Gabriel).

We ask this in the name of Jesus, our brother.
R. Amen.

(The "Rite of Confirmation")

(3) Human experience to be considered: giftedness   35 minutes

To begin this step of the process and stimulate discussion, the catechist reads "The Three Languages" from the Brothers Grimm.[7] This is the story of a young man whose father forces him out of the house to study and make something of himself. However, after three attempts the son is only able to learn the languages spoken by dogs, birds and frogs. Disgusted, the father believes the son is a failure, but the son eventually uses his unique gift to save others from danger. Child psychologist Bruno Bettelheim characterizes this fairy tale as "if it could have been written for the adolescent of today about his conflicts with his parents, or about parents' inability to understand what moves their adolescent children."[8]

The catechist emphasizes the young man's gift and how he uses it to help others. After reading the story, the catechist begins the large-group discussion by asking the following or similar questions (see **Fasting**):

What kind of relationship does the son have with his father?
Why is the son cast out?
What do you think the three animals—dogs, birds and frogs—symbolize? Why?
What gift(s) does the son have?
How does he use his gift(s)?

19

How do other people help him discover his gift(s)?
Have you had similar experiences? Can you share them?
What gift(s) do you have that you may have overlooked or considered trivial?
Is it necessary to leave home when searching for your gift(s)?
How did fasting help you in discerning your gift(s)?

Since this is a story about rebellion against parental authority and psychological separation, it may not ring true for young women. In this case, another fairy tale, story, video or drama may be used. There are countless fairy tales involving the giftedness and individuation of females ("Brother and Sister," "The Goose Girl," "Snow White," "Cinderella"), as well as myths and Native American tales.[9] Also, recent video releases like *Little Women* and *Sense and Sensibility* are excellent examples of giftedness among young women. If clips or excerpts from these alternatives are chosen, the catechist prepares new questions for the group discussion.

(4) Shared faith reflection   25 minutes

Males

The catechist introduces the story of Jeremiah's call (Jer 1:4–10) and asks everyone to get comfortable and listen attentively. It would be helpful to study a biblical commentary (e.g., *New Jerome Biblical Commentary)* for a brief overview of the political turmoil during this time (600 B.C.E.) and the ensuing Babylonian captivity. Jeremiah's initial reaction to God's call is noteworthy (as is Mary's in the Annunciation—Lk 1:26–38), and the youth should have no trouble identifying with it.

After reading the story, the catechist begins the discussion by asking the following questions:

Why does God call Jeremiah?
What is Jeremiah's reaction?
Why does he react this way?
What is he supposed to do?
How will Jeremiah's age affect his mission?
How will adults react to him?
What gift(s) does Jeremiah have?
Does he recognize his own gifts? Why/why not?
Are there any similarities between this story and "The Three Languages"?
    The Prodigal Son?
Is there a connection between this story and your own experience?

Females

The catechist introduces the Annunciation story in the same way, emphasizing Mary's age and the overwhelming experience of the visit. The miracle of the event consists in God's call *and* Mary's response to that call. The following or similar questions will help stimulate discussion.

Why does the angel Gabriel call Mary favored, saying that God is with her?

Why is she afraid?

Does Mary believe Gabriel?

Does she have any doubts?

Would you have any doubts?

How will Joseph, her family and others react to the news?

How can you recognize God's call?

What does it take to say *yes* to that call?

What gift(s) does Mary receive or discover?

What similarities exist between "The Three Languages" and Mary's experience?

(5) Acting justly   25 minutes

The catechist divides everyone into groups of three to five and asks them to share about their gifts for ten minutes. Afterward, each small group chooses a member to report briefly on their discussion. Then the catechist helps the large group decide how they will use their gifts for the benefit of the entire parish/school community. The catechist reminds everyone of the upcoming medicine walk and how it can help them discern gifts.

(6) Closing prayer   15 minutes

As in session one, the catechist uses different closing prayers for males and females. The purpose of the prayer is to express and share the giftedness of each individual. The giftedness of the group as a whole will be celebrated in the closing prayer of the third session on belonging.

Males

Gathering activity: By this time the catechist should have identified musicians in the group. The catechist invites these youth to play for the gathering activity, which involves youth coming together around the prayer center for chanting and/or song. The music should be within a suitable range for young men. Drumming, chanting and group dance may also be used. *Adult team members participate in the activity.*

Reading: When the gathering activity ends, a youth lights the candle(s) in the prayer center and another reads a portion of the scripture from the shared faith reflection. Example: Jer 1:6–8.

Reader: "The Word of the Lord."
  R.   "Thanks be to God."

Response to the reading: Youth stand in silence while instrumental music or drumming plays in the background. This should last no longer than three minutes.

Petitions: Petitions may be made by anyone in the group.

Leader: "Gift-giver, touch our lips and put your words in our mouths. For this we pray."
  R.   "Lord, hear our prayer."

Our Father: Everyone prays together in the circle, holding hands or hugging. This may be recited or sung.

Ritual action: This action is an exchange of peace that the leader introduces by saying, "Father, we remind each other of what you told Jeremiah: *Do not fear any-one*." The youth exchange a sign of peace with the same response.

Closing song: Since this corresponds to the liminal stage of the rite, the closing music should be subdued and prayerful (e.g., "On Eagles' Wings," "As the Deer Longs," "Envía Tu Espiritu").

Females

Gathering activity: At this stage the gathering activity should include group movement. The music should be soft and, if possible, performed with stringed or woodwind instruments. As with the males, the catechist invites musicians from the group to play.

Reading: When the activity ends, someone lights the candle in the prayer center and another youth reads Lk 1:35–38.

    Reader: "The Word of the Lord."

        R: "Thanks be to God."

Response to the reading: Youth stand silently in a circle and then recite or sing "We believe in the Word made flesh, God's presence in the world."[9]

Petitions: The response to each petition is "Mary, our sister, pray for us."

Our Father: This is said or sung in a circle with the youth holding hands or hugging.

Ritual action: Two youth remove a jar or small bowl of perfumed oil from the prayer table and anoint each other on the forehead with the sign of the cross saying, *Nothing is impossible with God* (Lk 1:37). They pass the oil around until everyone is anointed.

Closing song: Similar to the gathering activity. Liminal stage atmosphere should be subdued and prayerful (e.g., Miriam Therese Winter, *Breath of God* [Philadelphia, Pa.: Medical Mission Sisters, 1987]).

10. PARTICIPANTS' RESOURCES: See session one.

11. EVALUATION:

The leadership team fills out the first evaluation.

Please rate how well the catechetical session on giftedness met the following objectives for youth, (1) low (4) high:

(1)	Created a sense of community	1	2	3	4
(2)	Helped youth discover their gifts	1	2	3	4
(3)	Related scripture to giftedness	1	2	3	4
(4)	Formed a group commitment for using gifts	1	2	3	4
(5)	Expressed giftedness in ritual prayer	1	2	3	4

- What was the best part of the session?
- What needs to be improved?

- How prepared was the team in organizing/leading the session?
- Was the team helpful and present to youth? Why/why not?
- What changes should be made for the next session?
  Comments/Suggestions:

Youth fill out the second evaluation.

Please rate how well tonight's catechetical session on giftedness did in the following areas, (1) low (4) high:

(1)	Created a sense of community	1	2	3	4
(2)	Helped you discover your gifts	1	2	3	4
(3)	Related scripture to giftedness	1	2	3	4
(4)	Formed a group commitment to using gifts	1	2	3	4
(5)	Expressed giftedness in ritual prayer	1	2	3	4

- What did you learn at tonight's session?
- What did you like best?
- What would you change/add/delete?
  Comments/Suggestions:

SESSION THREE: BELONGING

1. PURPOSE OF GATHERING:

The third catechetical session builds on the previous sessions by leading youth toward a group identity and sense of belonging. It does this by helping them identify with a larger community (as Christian young men/women). It also explores ways for them to express their group identity. This part of the rite corresponds to reintegration into the community.

2–4. As in session two, these items (time, environment and profile of candidates) remain the same. See BACKGROUND of chapter one for details.

5. LIFE SIGN:

Erik Erikson devoted considerable time and study to the subject of belonging in identity-formation. He believed that belonging is one of the toughest challenges youth face and that they derive individual identity from membership in a group. Group membership forces youth to come out of the self-absorption of adolescence through relationships with peers and other people. Belonging to something greater than themselves gives males the challenge and females the relationships they need for socialization into the larger community.

6. BIBLICAL SIGN:

The account of the two disciples on the road to Emmaus (Lk 24:13–35) will be used as the biblical sign for the shared faith reflection for both males and females. There are four reasons for choosing this passage. First, the story takes place on the road with the two disciples walking from Jerusalem to Emmaus. This reinforces the idea of pilgrimage and will allow youth to talk about their experiences on the medicine walk. Second, verses 27–32 are key to the catechetical process, since the disciples take the initiative in asking Jesus to remain with them. Their eventual "discovery" results from something *they* had to do. Third, the account fits nicely into stages: separation (13–16); liminal period during which Jesus instructs the disciples (17–32); and reintegration (33–35). And last, Emmaus is a *story* rather than expository writing and will have greater impact on listeners during the session.

7. OBJECTIVES:

The objectives of the third catechetical session on belonging are:

(1) to deepen friendships among youth through a "buddy system,"

(2) to create a sense of belonging to the larger group,

(3) to show the importance of belonging in scripture,

(4) to prepare for the pilgrimage,

(5) to bond through ritual prayer.

8. CATECHIST REFLECTION:

Much of the work up to now has focused on the individual. Catechetical sessions, journaling, fasting and the medicine walk dealt with individual challenges and gifts. In this session, youth learn that they are part of a larger community from which they derive identity. This is important not just in psychological terms, but theologically. The Catholic faith tradition emphasizes the covenantal relationship between God and God's people. Individuals exercise free will and strive for a deeper relationship with Jesus, but they do this in the context of the community, the Body of Christ.

Many people want to belong to something greater than themselves. For youth, the need to commit themselves to an ideal or cause (Erikson's fidelity) is a powerful drive. This session offers them an opportunity to acknowledge and express that drive by moving from individual to communal identity based on Jesus Christ. Thus, it differs from the Native American vision quest and similar rituals described in **Catechist Resources.** This session also prepares youth for the pilgrimage, which is the outer expression of their inner transformation.

9. PROCESS OF CATECHESIS:

(1) Welcoming   10 minutes
As in previous sessions, the leadership team leads youth into the meeting room with the Easter candle. As they enter, youth place symbols from their medicine

walk in the prayer center. These include *meaningful* items discovered on the walk prior to the session. Musical accompaniment and singing help to create an atmosphere of welcome, which should be upbeat and lively.

(2) Gathering prayer

A team member burns incense and the prayer leader says the following prayer:

> *God of pilgrims and wanderers,*
> *You raised Jesus from darkness*
> *and gave hope to those who loved him.*
>
> *Stay with us this night*
> *and open our eyes to your presence.*
>
> *We make this prayer through Jesus our brother.*
> **R. Amen.**

(3) Human experience to be considered: belonging   45 minutes

The catechist invites youth to sit down and make themselves comfortable. Then he or she introduces the topic of belonging by reminding them that they are part of a larger parish/school/church. The catechist shows a segment of the 1993 movie *Swing Kids,* which portrays a group of young Bohemians living in Berlin during the 1930s. The catechist should preview the movie to determine the best scenes to show.

If desired, another video may be used, or the catechist can invite someone from the faith community to give compelling testimony. The catechist should check recent video releases dealing with coming-of-age and belonging, such as *White Squall* and *Little Women.* A list of films appears in Robert C. Hinkel, "Transition Films: A Selected Filmography," in *Betwixt & Between: Patterns of Masculine and Feminine Initiation,* 489–98.

Based on the segment shown, the catechist asks the following or similar questions:

What did you see? hear? feel?
What was going on in the scene?
Who are the "Swing Kids"?
What role does swing music play in their lives?
What changes occur among them?
Why are they attracted to the Hitler Youth Movement?
What does "Swing Heil" mean?
Why does Arvid commit suicide?
What happens to the main character?
What does the movie say about belonging?
What does it say about societal/peer pressure?

After the large-group discussion, the catechist asks youth to answer one or all of the following questions in their journals: "To what groups do I belong?" "Who are my friends?" "To what am I committed?" "What do I believe in?" "What do I fear?" Then the catechist divides them into groups of three or four and asks them to share their answers. The groups may be different from previous sessions so that youth have a chance to dialogue with new people.

(4) Shared faith reflection   25 minutes

The catechist introduces the Emmaus story (Lk 24:13–35). This is now the second (or third) story the youth have heard involving travel on the road. For males, the catechist emphasizes the importance of physical separation in coming to understand one's gifts and blessings. Without this distancing, self-discovery becomes more difficult. For females, the catechist highlights self-discovery in and through community. After reading the story, the catechist begins the discussion by asking the following or similar questions (see **Medicine Walk**):

What prevents the two disciples from recognizing Jesus?
What expectations did they have of Jesus of Nazareth?
Did events in Jerusalem meet their expectations?
Why do they invite Jesus to stay with them?
How do they finally recognize him?
What gifts do these two disciples have?
Do they recognize their own gifts?
Why do they return to Jerusalem "that same hour"?

26

Why does this story take place on the road?

Are there any similarities between this story and your medicine walk?

(5) Acting justly   20 minutes

The catechist asks youth to choose a "buddy" for the pilgrimage and mystagogia session. The adult team helps them pair up, making sure everyone has a buddy. In case of odd numbers or personality clashes, team members may pair up with youth. Each pair of buddies discusses the question "What prevents me from seeing Christ?" Then, in the large group, the catechist leads a discussion identifying the obstacles the entire community faces trying to see and do the work of Christ. Then they brainstorm ways in which *they* can help the community. This must be more than an academic exercise—the youth need to commit to some kind of action!

(6) Closing prayer   15 minutes

The purpose of this closing prayer is for youth to bond through ritual action.

Males

Gathering activity: Music for the gathering should be instrumental and familiar to everyone. If drumming is used, it should be different from previous sessions and invite group movement such as dancing, swaying or huddling.

Reading: A youth lights the candle(s) in the prayer center, a second one burns incense and a third proclaims Lk 24:31–33a.

Reader: "The Gospel of the Lord."

R.   "Praise to you, Lord Jesus Christ."

Response to the reading: The same gathering music/drumming plays as the prayer leader, a youth, retrieves a wooden bowl from the prayer center containing perfumed oil. He signs the feet of his buddy with the words: *That same hour they returned to Jerusalem.* Then the bowl is passed around the circle so that everyone gets signed.

Petitions: The leader begins after a moment of silence.

Leader: "God of pilgrims, be with us as we return to our community. For this we pray."

R.   "Lord, hear our prayer."

Our Father: Everyone prays together in the circle, holding hands or hugging. This may be recited or sung.

Ritual action: One at a time, the youth exchange symbols from the medicine walk with their buddies.

Closing song: Same as the gathering activity. Alternatives include reciting the Nicene Creed or renewing baptismal promises.

Females

Gathering activity: This may be a sung activity that includes group movement such as dance, signing or mime.

Reading: Lk 24:31–33a.

Response to the reading: The youth stand in silence for several minutes and then recite verse 31 three times, with their eyes closed: *Then their eyes were opened and they recognized him.*

Note: *Compare this to the reading from the Circle Dance (especially Is 6:5b—"My eyes have seen the King, the LORD of hosts!").*

Petitions:

Leader: "God of light, open our eyes so that we recognize Christ. For this we pray."

R.   "Mary, our sister, pray for us."

Our Father: This is recited or sung in a circle with everyone holding hands or hugging.

Ritual action: One at a time, youth exchange symbols from the medicine walk with their buddies. Then they massage each other's feet with perfumed oil from the prayer center. This is symbolic preparation for the pilgrimage.

Closing song: Similar to the gathering activity.

10. PARTICIPANTS' RESOURCES: See session one.

11. EVALUATION:

The leadership team fills out the first evaluation.

Please rate how well the catechetical session on belonging met the following objectives for youth, (1) low (4) high:

(1)	Encouraged friendships through a "buddy system"	1	2	3	4
(2)	Created a sense of belonging	1	2	3	4
(3)	Showed the importance of belonging in scripture	1	2	3	4
(4)	Prepared youth for the pilgrimage	1	2	3	4
(5)	Bonded youth through ritual prayer	1	2	3	4

- What was the best part of the session?
- What needs to be improved?
- How prepared was the team in organizing/leading the session?
- Was the team helpful and present to youth? Why/why not?
  Comments/Suggestions:

Youth fill out the second evaluation.

Please rate how well tonight's catechetical session on belonging did in the following areas, (1) low (4) high:

(1)	Encouraged friendships through a "buddy system"	1	2	3	4
(2)	Created a sense of belonging	1	2	3	4
(3)	Showed the importance of belonging in scripture	1	2	3	4

(4)	Prepared youth for the pilgrimage	1	2	3	4
(5)	Bonded youth through ritual prayer	1	2	3	4

- What did you learn from tonight's session?
- What did you like best?
- What did you like least?
  Comments/Suggestions:

CHAPTER TWO

This chapter contains the Circle Dance, the pilgrimage and a mystagogia session. As in the previous chapter, the catechesis follows Mongoven's process but should be adapted to meet local needs and circumstances. The catechist should refer to the **Catechist Resources** at the back of the book. An entire ritual is presented in the Circle Dance, which is the first time males and females come together in the rite. For reasons of identity formation, they should go through the catechetical sessions separately and not mix. The pilgrimage presented here outlines the process to be followed, but the catechist needs to do much of the hands-on work (site selection, route, team job descriptions, medical/release forms, permission slips, equipment list, liturgy preparation, etc.). It is best to assemble a manual containing information under each of these areas with different team members responsible for each area.

Again, the pilgrimage should reflect the local church and needs of the particular group of pilgrims. The mystagogia session follows the catechetical process in chapter one.

THE CIRCLE DANCE

The Circle Dance brings males and females together *ritually* in a way that is complementary. The dance takes the form of the closing prayer in the catechetical sessions, which is an abbreviated Liturgy of the Hours, except that the *Our Father* and *ritual action* are reversed. Ideally, the site for the dance should be away from the parish/school, and the dance should be performed either in the early morning or evening. Youth may suggest sites from their medicine walk and fast, which were done in preparation for the dance.

After everyone assembles, the catechist and team distribute bandannas (red for males; yellow for females), which will be worn during the pilgrimage. If needed, scarves or sashes may be used to avoid a gang look.

Gathering: The catechist or Circle Dance leader lights a fire, and the youth form two circles (females on the inside; males on the outside). Drums, flutes and/or string instruments may be played as they gather. If a musical "theme" has been used throughout the catechetical sessions, then it should be repeated. If not, liturgical songs may be used (e.g., "Sing A New Song," "Alabaré," "Lord of the Dance"). Youth lock arms and sing as they gather.

Blessing: The leader begins by blessing the fire with these words:

Creator God,

In the beginning
you dispelled the darkness
with the fire of the sun,
which gives warmth to every
creature on earth.

You led your chosen people
out of the wilderness
with a pillar of fire,
and sent down fire
to consume Elijah's offering.

You sent your Spirit
to the upper room to rest
on your Son's disciples
in tongues of fire.

We ask you to bless this fire
as you bless us
with the fire of your love,
and as we gather to praise your name.
R. Amen.

Reading: Pause. Then a youth reads Is 6:1–8.

Response to Reading: Youth respond to the reading by chanting the following exchange three times:

Males: "Whom shall I send?"

Females: "Who will go for us?"

All: "Here I am, send me!"

Again the music plays, and both circles dance around the fire in opposite directions.

Ritual action: Once the music stops a youth burns incense on the fire, and the catechist or dance leader conducts the litany of Ps 136 (vv. 1–9; 13–16; 23–26). The response ("God's love endures forever") is recited or sung by all youth.

After the litany, the females turn and face the males. The males approach them, exchange bandannas or sashes and then trade places. Now the females are on the outside with red bandannas, and the males are on the inside with yellow ones. Instrumental music (drumming) plays again, and both circles move around the fire *twice* in opposite directions. When the music stops they face each other, exchange bandannas again and form one large circle with the adults.

Our Father: Everyone holds hands in a large circle.

Closing song: This may be the same as the gathering music. It should be appropriate for a liturgical celebration and contain a sending or commissioning theme (e.g., "Here I Am, Lord," "Be Not Afraid," "Caminaré").

Note: *The catechist/team should be prepared to handle gender and sexuality issues, which are an integral part of the identity-formation process. If youth have not asked questions or raised the topic before, they are likely to do so now. This is a natural development, and the catechist should deal with the theme openly and honestly. Team members play a crucial role by acting as role models and mentors to youth. They can help answer questions such as: "How am I supposed to act as an adult male/female?" "How do I relate to others of the same/opposite sex?" "How is my sexuality related to my faith?" "What does the church teach about sexuality?" "What does society and the media say about sexuality?" "What is the difference between sexuality and sex?" See chapter seven, "Adolescence, Sexuality, and Spiritual Growth" in Charles Shelton's* Adolescent Spirituality.

PILGRIMAGE

The pilgrimage is done as any overnight pilgrimage or retreat would be done. The catechist should consult the **Catechist Resources** as well as local sources of information—other parishes, the diocesan office, community youth programs like the "Ropes" course, wilderness adventure clubs, the Sierra Club, backpacking and hiking manuals and Jean Dalby Clift and Wallace B. Clift's *The Archetype of Pilgrimage: Outer Action with Inner Meaning* (New York: Paulist Press, 1996). The pilgrimage will come as a surprise and even an interruption in the flow of the rite after the ordered, ritualized catechetical sessions and Circle Dance. This is as it should be. With all its dust, heat, glare, sweat and demands, the pilgrimage is the actual, physical manifestation of inner change. Pilgrims must work hard to participate in it, or the rite will lose much of its benefit.

1. PREPARATION:

The catechist schedules a meeting before the pilgrimage to review basics of hiking, camping, first-aid and fasting. As mentioned previously, the catechist should create a manual for the rite containing job descriptions for each team member. At least one member should have backpacking, hiking and/or camping experience. Another team member should have first-aid training and carry emergency supplies, as well as medical insurance and health forms. The team also reviews the goals of the pilgrimage, site information, agenda and an equipment list with each other, the pilgrims and any concerned parents/guardians.

2. OBJECTIVES:

The pilgrimage has three objectives:

(1) to strengthen friendships formed in the catechetical sessions,

(2) to give pilgrims a chance to wrestle with any personal issues,

(3) to give pilgrims a new name based on their wilderness experience.

The adult team may suggest ways for pilgrims to meet these objectives such as on-going journaling, walking the pilgrimage route with their buddies and reading scripture passages in preparation for the pilgrimage. In addition to the scriptures used in the catechetical sessions, pilgrims may find the following passages helpful: Jacob wrestling the angel (Gn 32:22–32); Ruth and Naomi (Ru); Elijah fleeing to Mount Horeb (1 Kgs 19:1–13a); Judith defeating the Assyrians (Jdt); Esther's struggle against Haman (Est); Ezekiel and the dried bones (Ez 37:1–14); Jesus in the desert (Mt 4:1–11); the Syrophoenician woman (Mk 7:24–30); and any of the Lucan parables (e.g., the sower 8:4–8; the Good Samaritan 10:30–37; the mustard seed 13:18–19; the lost sheep 15:1–7; Lazarus and the rich man 16:19–31; the rich young man 18:18–30; Zacheus 19:1–9).

3. SITE:

Distance lends perspective. Therefore, the site should be far from the parish or school and relate in some way to the church and Christian faith. A cathedral, church, mission, retreat house, college, seminary, monastery or convent may be used. However, the site does not have to be an actual pilgrimage center or connected with "official" symbols of church. The catechist and team may choose a mountain park, beach, nature trail, lodge, campground or other quiet place considered special. As stated in chapter three, the sacredness of the site derives from the gathering of pilgrims and team for the purpose of psychological and spiritual growth.

4. AGENDA:

Pilgrims and team assemble early in the morning for the bus/caravan ride to the pilgrimage site. Buddies help each other with provisions. The catechist leaves the itinerary and site information with appropriate school/parish staff, who act as the point of contact for parents and families back home.

Upon arrival at the site, the catechist or leader checks in and gives final instructions for the hike, which can range anywhere from 3 to 10 miles. After the hike, when youth and team arrive at the campout location, the buddies pair off by themselves to a secluded spot and prepare their campsite. They may have tents, although tents are not required. Buddies must then separate until bedtime, spending the time journaling, praying, sitting quietly and listening to the sounds of their new environment. They do not speak again until morning, when they divulge their names to each other. The team should check in with the buddies *at least once* before bedtime.

Listening for a new name requires considerable attention and focus on one's surroundings. It is best for youth to spend the night outside either on the church or mission grounds, with access to a chapel all night. As in the scripture passages cited previously and the American Indian vision quest, a new name is meant to reflect the inner identity of the individual. In the New Testament, Peter (Mt

34

16:17–19), Levi the tax collector (Mk 2:13–17) and Saul (Acts 13:9) assume names that signify their identities as disciples. The inspiration for a name can come from anywhere—a sound, vision, dream, thought, feeling or object sighted in the darkness. Adult team members should consult the vision quest material listed in **Catechist Resources** and be available for pilgrims during the night.

Note: The name does not necessarily have to be new but may be a rediscovery or appreciation of a given name, surname or confirmation name. The catechist may also provide material on the lives of the saints as examples and models of Christian living and conversion. If youth assume saints' names, they should understand the difference between this rite and confirmation.

In the morning everyone assembles for a dawn liturgy at the base camp. The pilgrims may give testimonies of their experience during the night, read from their journals or talk about their new names. The catechist/leader should arrange transportation back home. If a welcoming ceremony or meal is planned, it should be done soon after arrival at the parish/school. Pilgrims should be encouraged to share their experiences publicly with family, friends and guests (see Closing Prayer of mystagogia session and *From Age to Age: The Challenge of Worship with Adolescents,* published by the National Federation for Catholic Youth Ministry).

5. EQUIPMENT LIST:

The basic list for materials follows. The catechist/leader/team members may change or add to this list to fit the particular needs of their group. No electronic device like a radio, Walkman, or hair dryer is allowed. Neither is alcohol or illegal drugs. Snacks may be brought on the pilgrimage only for consumption after the liturgy.

Recommended equipment list:

Bible
journal
pens/pencils
backpack
sleeping bag
sleeping pad
toilet paper
knife
sunscreen
insect repellent
baseball cap/visor
flashlight
matches
bandanna/sash
water and/or juices (at least half a gallon per person)
ground cloth or rain tarp
warm clothes
hiking boots

wool cap
jacket
whistle (for emergencies only)
musical instrument(s)

MYSTAGOGIA SESSION

1. PURPOSE OF GATHERING:

Traditionally, mystagogia has referred to the post-baptismal catechesis within the catechumenate. In the fourth and fifth centuries, mystagogues such as Cyril of Jerusalem, John Chrysostom, Ambrose of Milan and Theodore of Mopsuestia catechized the newly-initiated Christians using rich imagery from salvation history. Today, mystagogia refers more to an appreciation of the mystery and presence of God in all human acts and is not confined to the period immediately following baptism.

The mystagogia session is an essential part of the rite of passage. Its purpose is to allow youth to share their experiences and interpret them in the light of scripture. It also gives closure to the rite. As in the Circle Dance, the *Our Father* and *ritual action* are reversed.

Note: Parents, friends, priests, teachers and parishioners should be invited to the closing prayer and social at the end of this session.

2–4. These remain the same in the mystagogia session as for the other sessions. See BACKGROUND of chapter one for details.

5. LIFE SIGN:

The life sign or human experience to be considered in this session is "ending." This is an experience that the youth will encounter many times in their lives, and they need to be prepared for it. Without closure, meaningful events and relationships in their lives may not reach their fullness. Bringing closure to an initiation process is crucial, because it gives youth permission to move on and mature. They may now enter the world of adulthood with a little less guilt, doubt and fear. Ideally, males will feel that they have "passed the test," and females will form relationships that will last even through adulthood.

6. BIBLICAL SIGN:

The biblical sign for the shared faith reflection is the resurrection of Jesus (Mk 16:1–8). Mark's account of the resurrection contains mystery, surprise and uncertainty. The women who go to the tomb to anoint Jesus' body find the stone rolled away and a "young man dressed in white robes" inside. He tells them, "He is not here. He is resurrected." Frightened, they leave the tomb unsure of what they have witnessed, and so they tell no one. This is similar to what youth may experience in real life, since closure rarely has absolute certainty to it.

7. OBJECTIVES:

The objectives of the mystagogia session are:

(1)   to deepen friendships among the pilgrims,

(2)   to enable youth to share their experiences of the pilgrimage,

(3)   to seek the wisdom of scripture in interpreting significant events,

(4)   to motivate youth to participate in parish/school ministries,

(5)   to pray as a community of adults.

8. CATECHIST REFLECTION:

This mystagogia session is the fourth and final part of *Pilgrimage as Rite of Passage.* Its purpose is to allow youth to share their experiences and interpret them biblically. This corresponds to the reintegration stage of initiation and is extremely important as a means of confirming Christian identity. The name they have chosen or received for themselves must be accepted first by their group and then by the larger parish/school community. This legitimizes their newly-discovered gifts and serves as a welcome into the adult Christian world.

The way youth interpret their experience is crucial to the success of the rite. Some may still harbor doubts about themselves, the process, the value of the pilgrimage and whether they truly are adults. They may or may not feel different, which can lead to even greater confusion. This is the reason for the passage from Mark. The women experience the resurrection and are so disturbed by it they do not mention a word to anyone. Youth may feel the same way. The mystagogia session allows them to share their feelings and interpret them in a way that the women in Mark's Gospel apparently do not.

Lastly, the session encourages pilgrims to continue their relationships with each other and get involved in parish/school activities. This includes social justice projects, youth and young adult ministry, catechetics, tutoring, liturgical ministries and community-based programs. The catechist and team should be available after the session for counseling or group activities. This will provide a sense of continuity to the rite and diminish any hint of graduation. The youth have not graduated *from* something but have been initiated *into* greater involvement in the community.

9. PROCESS OF CATECHESIS:

(1) Welcoming   10 minutes
The catechist, adult team and pilgrims assemble in the meeting room. Suggested gathering activity is for everyone to introduce themselves by their new names (if this has not been done previously) and then autograph each other's journals. The catechist and team should have journals of their own and can join the youth in signing.

(2) Gathering prayer
A youth leads the group in the opening prayer adapted from the "Rite of Confirmation."

Lord,
you renamed Abram, Simon and Saul
Abraham, Peter and Paul.
Call us now by our new names and
help us witness to the Risen Christ
who lives and reigns with you and the Holy Spirit,
one God, for ever and ever.
R. Amen.

(3) Human experience to be considered: closure   35 minutes

The catechist takes this time to make some general observations about the pilgrimage and any necessary announcements. Then he or she asks the following questions:

What happened on the pilgrimage?
Did you find it hard or easy?
What was the best part?
What was the worst part?
How did you get along with your buddy?
Were you able to journal, read or pray?
What distracted you?
Did you overcome the distractions? How?
What did you learn during the pilgrimage?
What did you discover about yourself?
What did you discover about your relationships?
What did you discover about God?

The catechist also invites youth to comment on the catechetical sessions to see how males/females approached the rite differently. They should have an opportunity to talk about the pilgrimage from the perspective of gender. Once they have shared their experiences, the catechist and team may answer the same or similar questions. Comments on how *individuals* performed during the rite and/or pilgrimage should be brief and affirming.

4) Shared faith reflection   25 minutes

Another youth reads Mk 16:1–8. The catechist asks the following questions, which relate the pilgrimage to the resurrection experience described in the reading.

What are the women thinking about on the way to the tomb?
What do they do when they arrive?
Why are they afraid?
What does the youth tell them?
What do the women do upon leaving?
Why are they "seized with trembling and bewilderment"?
What were you thinking about on the pilgrimage?
What did you do when you finished?

Was the night outside like going into a tomb? How?
What did you hear/see/feel?

(5) Acting justly   20 minutes

This is the time for youth to make a commitment to the parish/school community. The catechist invites someone such as a pastor, priest, youth or campus minister, community leader or someone who uses a community service to talk about the needs and opportunities of the larger community. After the presentation, youth may sign up for different ministries. They should also commit to helping one another and staying in touch with their buddies. Buddies may volunteer for ministries together.

(6) Closing prayer   25 minutes

The same closing prayer is used for males and females. *It should be planned and carried out by a team of male and female pilgrims with help from adults.* The group leaves the meeting room in procession behind the Easter candle and gathers in the church building, chapel or other site. Guests such as parents, relatives and friends are already assembled. A youth leads the prayer.

Gathering: This may be similar to the gathering music done throughout the catechetical sessions but should be sung music appropriate for liturgy and familiar to guests (e.g., "City of God," "Vienen con Alegría," etc.). The prayer leader should make a special effort to welcome everyone, especially guests, to the celebration.

Reading: Another youth reads the entire passage from Mark's Gospel (16:1–8)

Response to the reading: Any number of responses would be appropriate, including kneeling for at least one minute in silence, singing/chanting a psalm or listening to soft drumming or similar music from the catechetical sessions. The catechist/team should try to *assist* the youth planning the liturgy.

Petitions: Youth are responsible for writing and reciting the petitions. The petitions include prayers for the universal church, the RCIA, the sick and dying, the needs of the local parish/school, the youth, their families and the adult team leaders. The response may be sung.

Ritual action: The catechist steps to the front of the assembly, giving a *brief* report on the pilgrimage. Then he or she calls the youth forward by his or her new name. Each person gives a one- or two-line explanation of its meaning. A parent, friend or relative then presents the pilgrim with a red or yellow rose as a symbol of achievement. When they have finished, the assembly welcomes them by applauding, and the youth return to their places.

Our Father: Everyone prays holding hands.

Note: *This is an ideal time for personal testimony from the youth, which allows them to assume adult roles publicly. If done, the testimonies should be brief.*

Closing song: Similar to the gathering activity.

After the closing prayer the catechist/team should prepare a meal in honor of the pilgrims to which all are invited. Those who help in preparing and serving the meal may be parents, relatives, teachers, youth or campus ministers, parish associations and individual parishioners.

11. PARTICIPANTS' RESOURCES: See session one.

12. EVALUATION:

The leadership team meets after the mystagogia session and fills out the following evaluation. The catechist and team meet again one to two weeks after the session to evaluate the entire rite and make recommendations for the following year. Particular emphasis should be given to the pilgrimage at that time. Also, the team should evaluate their own participation in the rite. The catechist can recognize these volunteers with a certificate, a dinner or similar function. The team may want to report the results of the rite (bilingually) to the entire parish/school either through announcements, meetings or bulletins.

Please rate how well you think the mystagogia session met the following objectives for youth, (1) low, (4) high:

(1)	Deepened friendships among youth	1	2	3	4
(2)	Shared experiences of pilgrimage	1	2	3	4
(3)	Sought the wisdom of scripture	1	2	3	4
(4)	Encouraged community involvement	1	2	3	4
(5)	Prayed as a community of adults	1	2	3	4

- What was the best part of the session?
- What needs to be improved?
- How prepared was the team?
- Was the team present and helpful to youth? Their families? The parish/school?
- Why/why not?
- How would you describe the involvement of parents/friends/guests?

Youth fill out the following evaluation. This is an important evaluation, and the catechist should allow enough time for the group to complete it. Note that it includes questions about the Circle Dance and Pilgrimage. This assumes that neither one has been evaluated yet. If the catechist has a chance to ask these questions beforehand, he or she should do so.

Please rate how well you think the mystagogia session met the following objectives, (1) low (4) high:

(1)	Deepened friendships among youth	1	2	3	4
(2)	Shared experiences of pilgrimage	1	2	3	4
(3)	Sought the wisdom of scripture	1	2	3	4
(4)	Encouraged community involvement	1	2	3	4
(5)	Prayed as a community of adults	1	2	3	4

- What was the best part of this session? Why?
- What did you think of the Circle Dance?
- What would you change?
- Was the pilgrimage what you expected? Why/why not?
- What would you change?
- Are you interested in helping in some way next year? If yes, please include your phone number.

CHAPTER THREE

The death of rock star Kurt Cobain of the group *Nirvana* sent shock waves throughout the music world. Thousands of followers of the 27-year-old Cobain, who committed suicide with a handgun in his Seattle home in 1994, mourned his death as a tragedy not just for the rock music world, but for themselves personally. Cobain had become a symbol of their despair and hopelessness, and his lyrics offered a sense of identity they could find nowhere else in society.

The type of music Cobain played is known as "grunge" rock, which deals with themes of death, self-destruction, violence, sex, obsession, and rebellion against an adult society viewed as meaningless and superficial. Grunge rockers and their followers typically wear flannel shirts, baggy pants, t-shirts and black military boots. They pierce their bodies with jewelry and tattoos, smoke tobacco and marijuana, drink booze, abuse drugs and rebel against authority.

Why the self-destructive, rebellious lifestyle? "Let this be clear," explains one grunge rocker. "We *hate* you."[11] The reason for such intense hatred directed at the older generation is equally clear. "What does your generation have to uniquely identify itself? Info-mercials, docudramas and Coca-Cola jingles. Yeah, you guys sure have changed the world," states the same grunge rocker in a fiery letter to the editor of the *San Francisco Chronicle*.[12]

This attitude has led some adults to accuse these youth of having no purpose, no reason for being and no way to identify themselves. Life for many in this generation—including adolescents—has become a lost cause, and many have opted out of an adult world they find out-of-reach and meaningless.

ERIK ERIKSON'S THEORY OF PSYCHOLOGICAL DEVELOPMENT

Writing during the social revolution of the sixties with its peace protests, drug experiments and free sex, Erik H. Erikson developed a theory of psychological development that speaks directly to the disillusion of youth today. It is based on the idea of life as a cycle or process. According to Erikson, as people grow older they pass through psychological stages with different characteristics and aspects of human growth. Each stage has a major task or conflict to be resolved before the individual passes on to the next phase. Not all individuals mature at the same rate; nor do we all reach the end of our lives as integrated, whole human beings.

In his research at Harvard University and elsewhere, Erikson found that the conflicts most people struggled with could be grouped into stages and that these stages represented archetypes of human development. He identified eight stages of development from infancy to old age, as well as the conflict in each stage that the individual must resolve in order to mature. If these conflicts are not resolved, the individual grows older chronologically, but becomes mired in the tension of an earlier stage.

The stages in Erikson's life cycle are: (1) infancy, (2) early childhood, (3) play age, (4) school age, (5) adolescence, (6) young adulthood, (7) adulthood and (8) old age.[13] Erikson believed that adolescence is the most important, because its sole task is *identity formation* and that without proper formation, moral and ethical development would be hindered.[14] He noted that the entire cycle "has its normative crisis in adolescence, and is in many ways determined by what went before and determines much that follows."[15]

In Erikson's theory, the great task of adolescence is to forge an identity that will guide and sustain the person through the difficult transition to adulthood and old age. If this is not done, or if previous stages have not been completed, development becomes blocked and *confusion* results in moral and ethical development. This may happen on the individual psychological level and in society at large.

ERIKSON'S THEORY OF IDENTITY FORMATION

Erikson believed that identity formation during adolescence is based on two major separations—the first from parental authority and the second from societal conventions. This is also the time when formal cognitive and reflective skills develop, both of which aid the separation process and give the adolescent some autonomy. This autonomy varies significantly with age, family, ethnic background, economic level and gender. Although Erikson's stages are concerned with the psychological development of individuals, social interaction is also important. This is especially true during adolescence, which is a time when the individual needs others to help establish an identity.

Erikson believed that youth need to view themselves through the eyes of others, and only in this way can they begin to put the pieces of their identity together. But this process is a two-way street. Just as society recognizes the need of youth to test limits, it wants to be recognized *by* youth as real and legitimate. This creates a dynamic relationship between the emerging adult and society. Erikson believed that a weakening of either side in this relationship offsets the balance and affects the growth of the individual and society.

But for many youth this sense of mutuality is beyond their grasp. Rather than feeling at home with their bodies, knowing where they are going in school and feeling support from the people in their lives who count, they experience the opposite. Thus, the great adventure of adolescence—testing oneself, pushing the limits and feeling one's potential—becomes an exercise in frustration and despair. Identity is not formed, because it has no way of testing itself in a competitive, technological environment.

If the three new sources of energy in youth—physical growth, intellectual development and genital maturation—are blocked or have no constructive way to express themselves, a sense of rage and despair develops.[16] This is the same rage that characterizes many of the underworld movements in youth culture such as grunge rock. It is certainly no coincidence that the name of the "thrash-funk" band Kurt Cobain's widow, Courtney Love, plays in is called *Faith No More.*

Erikson believed that at no other time in the life cycle was "the promise of finding oneself and the threat of losing oneself so closely allied" as in adolescence.[17] For this reason, the characteristic he termed *fidelity* is key to understanding identity formation and confusion. Fidelity is a personal commitment so profound as to give meaning and purpose to the individual making the commitment. For adolescents, the commitment usually means a certain way to dress, talk, walk, relate to others and interpret the world around them.

The individual youth spends much of adolescence searching for something and/or someone to believe in (an ideology). After much testing and soul-searching, the adolescent makes a commitment with tremendous passion and energy. In most cases this is done without their realizing that they are being formed not by the ideology, but by the *act* of commitment. This leads to a journey of self-discovery that affects the youth for the rest of the life cycle.

Writing about fidelity, theologian and liturgist Aidan Kavanagh has observed:

> …living "mythically" (i.e., within values rather than in a detached or "uncommitted" way in regard to those values) is rapidly becoming the life-style of youth, and constitutes the chasm separating it from older generations given more to rational discourse about reality than to enacting reality by engaging in it. Youth's alternative I regard as far and away the more human of the two and, for this reason, I am confident that it will prevail, that it has already in fact begun to do so, not only among youth but the population generally.[18]

But what about the youth who don't make it? For every journey of self-discovery that leads to a grounded sense of identity, there are many more that end in confusion. Erikson believed that identity confusion results from too great a gap between how individual youth view themselves and how society views them. If society offers no meaningful object for their fidelity, youth may squander their energy in delinquency, perversion or withdrawal.[19] Erikson called this *infidelity.* The increase in youth violence, gang activity, drive-by shootings and hate crimes seems to support this. And the constant cry of youth ministers, social workers and psychologists is that youth have nowhere to go and nothing to do. Society in the nineties has given them few options and seems uninterested in their plight.[20]

Erikson believed that during a crisis adolescents reevaluate their current values and behaviors and explore options regarding religious practice, sexuality, vocation and politics. Then they commit themselves to one or several of these choices. But he also identified a moratorium period: a time when the search for identity is put on hold or delayed. He attributed this to a natural reaction on the part of the psyche to protect the individual and prepare itself for the ensuing identity crisis. The moratorium period for today's youth is longer than in any previous generation because of the increased pressure and demands of modern-day existence.[21]

But even this moratorium involves conflict, because it represents a moment of transition. The adolescent recognizes a certain sameness and discontinuity between the inner self and society. Erikson likened it to that breathless moment when a trapeze artist must let go of one bar in order to reach another.[22] This letting go can be done only with *trust,* which forms the bedrock of all stages in the life cycle. Ironically, in his research Erikson discovered basic conflicts of trust still active in one form or another in many adults.

CAROL GILLIGAN: A DIFFERENT VOICE

Just as Erikson identified two major separations in the individuation process (from parental authority and societal conventions), Carol Gilligan of Harvard University discovered two major *connections.* The first is the discovery that other people have real needs and desires distinct from our own. The second, occurring during identity formation in adolescence, is the gradual disclosure of the inner self, which often has needs that remain unconscious until a crisis.[23] It is precisely at this moment of awakening that the adolescent needs the most care and support from family, friends, the faith community and teachers.

Until the late seventies, nearly all research on the psychological development of youth was done on males. Males formed the norm for many psychologists from Piaget to Kohlberg. The standard model described the qualities necessary for adulthood as masculine: autonomous, independent, separate, competitive, formal, abstract, individual. Gilligan characterizes this as a "propositional" or "justice model."[24] Here, justice refers to the abstract construction of rules and laws governing human behavior and moral decision-making. Erikson's belief that identity formation requires separation from parents and community reflects this justice model of male development.

In her groundbreaking book, *In A Different Voice: Psychological Theory and Women's Development,* Gilligan outlined a model of development very different from the justice model.[25] In studying the way girls and young women solve moral dilemmas, Gilligan discovered that their psychological development was nearly opposite to that of boys and young men. Rather than mature through a process of separation and replacement, she found that females mature through attachment and continuity, expanding their relationships both in number and depth. She termed this development a *model of care.*[26]

In her care model, Gilligan identified the qualities necessary for adulthood as: connectedness, continuity, responsibility to others, compassion, acceptance and loyalty. These traits move toward and have their center in relationships. An adolescent girl's identity is defined by the type and quality of her relationships. In contrast to male development, which is measured by the distance (both figuratively and literally) the adolescent puts between himself and other people, female development measures itself in proximity to others. According to Gilligan, the greatest unconscious fear of boys is intimacy—a loss of self viewed as disruptive to the process of separation begun in infancy. Girls, however, fear isolation and loneliness, which disrupt the process of bonding begun at birth.[27]

Gilligan described both of these developmental models as resulting in two very different moral and ethical perspectives: one of rights, the other of responsibility.

45

She concludes:

> The moral imperative that emerges repeatedly in interviews with women is an injunction to care, a responsibility to discern and alleviate the "real and recognizable trouble" of this world. For men, the moral imperative appears rather as an injunction to respect the rights of others and thus to protect from interference the rights to life and self-fulfillment. Women's insistence on care is at first self-critical rather than self-protective, while men initially conceive obligation to others negatively in terms of non-interference. Development for both sexes would therefore seem to entail an integration of rights and responsibilities through the discovery of the *complementarity* of these disparate views.[28]

Pilgrimage as Rite of Passage integrates these male and female perspectives described by Gilligan. She points out that in order to achieve integration, areas of "complementarity" must be found.[29] But complementarity should not be viewed as a mixture or amalgamation of male and female development. Rather, it must celebrate the uniqueness of the two models of development without watering down the essence of either. This is not impossible, for the goal of both is *identity*. The fact that boys and girls answer the question "Who am I?" in different ways does not mean they are incompatible. It shows the necessity of both male and female perspectives in coming to an integrated sense of self. Complementarity, by definition, involves relationship, and relationships lie at the heart of identity formation.

If these two developmental models are going to come together, then the meeting must take place as part of a group process. This is the only way the needs of both males and females can be fulfilled. But the concept of group goes beyond belonging to the same gender/age/geographical location/high school. It extends to everyone in the community: children, adults, seniors, those newly-arrived and the marginalized. For if complementarity exists between male and female in identity formation, it also exists throughout the entire life cycle.

There are moments when individuals at different stages of the cycle can help each other. Erikson's model is not individualistic but communal. The way the community passes through the stages of the life cycle is through ritual.[30] Erikson concluded: "Religion restores, at regular intervals and through rituals significantly connected with the important crises of the life cycle and the turning points of the yearly cycle, a new sense of wholeness, of things rebound."[31]

Novelist Wendell Berry describes one important crisis in the life of a young woman, who, unfortunately, did not survive the crisis.

Berry writes:

> I received a letter containing an account of a recent suicide: "My friend...jumped off the Golden Gate Bridge two months ago. She had been terribly depressed for years. There was no help for her. None that she could find that was sufficient. She was trying to get from one phase of her life to another, and couldn't make it...She destroyed herself."
>
> The letter had already asked, "How does a human pass through youth to maturity without breaking down?" And it had answered, "help from tradition, through ceremonies and rituals, rites of passage at the most difficult stages."[32]

THE NEED FOR RITUAL

For many people, "ritual" involves superficial, affected acts that have little or no meaning. The common view is to associate ritual with rote activities, going through the motions and secret societies or cults that have no place in modern society. As Mary Douglas argues in *Natural Symbols,* there is a widespread rejection of symbols and rituals today: "Ritual has become a bad word signifying empty conformity. We are witnessing a revolt against formalism, even against form."[33]

But what, exactly, is ritual? It has been described as something as simple as two children avoiding the cracks in the sidewalk, or two woodcutters working together, swinging their axes in rhythm.[34] In *The Meaning of Ritual,* Leonel Mitchell describes ritual as those acts that people do on a repetitive basis: blowing out candles on a birthday cake, champagne toast and kiss on New Year's Eve, the elaborate ceremonies and gatherings that have developed around the Olympic games and Super Bowl.[35]

In this sense, ritual is merely a description of what people do, but it can also be as expansive as humanity's response to the transcendent. For instance, Mitchell believes that ritual gives meaning and purpose to those participating in it. He notes: "One function of ritual in the present world is to give a sense of identity and community to those who would otherwise have none."[36] Therefore, ritual is not only an important part of identity, but of life. This is important because contemporary identity, according to Mitchell, comes not so much from *who* we *are,* but from *what* we *do.*

Fortunately, ritual thrives today in a multitude of forms. We engage in it from the early morning when we drink two cups of coffee and read the metro section of the newspaper before heading off to work, to the end of the day when we check the locks and turn out the lights before going to bed. Ritual permeates our lives, giving us something to do, a routine that allows us to engage the world in a way that is uniquely our own. Ritual is often regarded as personal as a set of fingerprints, which may explain the current rejection of communal forms.

But what happens once a ritual becomes irrelevant? "Relevance" is a slippery word. What is relevant today may not be relevant tomorrow, and so rituals change. Anthropologist Peter Berger has written extensively about modernity, the loss of connection to the supernatural in modern culture and the rise of secularization.[37] He argues that the triumph of the empirical, practical, scientific world over the transcendent, metaphysical, spiritual one has thrown society into a tailspin.[38] Much of humanity has lost meaning and purpose because it has lost sight of the larger issues—ones that many youth, in particular, are grappling with as they search for authenticity, something *real* to hold on to.

Triviality in modern life is exactly what grunge rockers and many other youth decry today. They are looking for answers to the questions posed by Berger, and they are willing to look almost anywhere to find them: religion, education, media, music, sports, drugs, gangs, violence. What they are *not* looking for (and what society seems all too eager to provide) is information about how to wear condoms, fill out credit reports and get that perfect body for summer.[39] These may be of importance at certain times, but they do not provide youth with the deep sense of confidence and joy that comes from knowing who they are, where they have come from and where they are going.

VAN GENNEP'S STAGES OF INITIATION

Initiation as a characteristic of human development is so important that cultural anthropologist Mircea Eliade called it "one of the most significant spiritual phenomena in the history of humanity"![40] He believed that initiation "is an act that involves not only the religious life of the individual, in the modern meaning of the word 'religion'; it involves his *entire* life."[41] Moreover, Leonel Mitchell has pointed out that, "In many languages the word for human being is the same as that for an initiated member of the tribe."[42]

Whether in tribes, communities or modern nations, initiation serves to transform the individual in several ways: from child to adult, from a non-sexual being to one who is sexually aware, from religious naivete to a spiritual vision.[43] But this transformation also affects the community since, as in Erikson's life cycle, the newly-initiated bring fresh energy and creativity into the larger community. Curiously, the movement or passing from one age group to another has been marked in very similar ways by cultures in Egypt, Syria, Ancient Greece, Asia, Native America, Africa and India.[44]

In his study of ritual behavior at the turn of the century, anthropologist Arnold van Gennep identified three stages common to all initiation ceremonies. These stages are: (1) separation from the former world, (2) transition to the new world, and (3) incorporation back into the tribe or community. Van Gennep called these stages a "rite of passage," which moves youth into the social, sexual and spiritual world of the adult community.[45] Youth who make the transition assume the corporate identity of the tribe/community/ethnic group but also retain a personal identity that distinguishes them from others in the group. Today, such rites either are in decline or have disappeared completely. But, according to Erikson, identity for youth can easily become confused or lost without well-defined initiation rites.[46]

Studying adolescent rites of passage in primitive societies, van Gennep found that the first stage—separation from the childhood world—was usually abrupt and even forceful. This was done in order to mark the difference between the two worlds and to let initiates know there was no turning back. Initiates, both boys and girls, had to give up their childhood ways and commit themselves to adulthood. More often than not, they were separated physically as well as emotionally from the rest of the community. Van Gennep recorded numerous accounts of native tribes isolating initiates for a considerable length of time as a way to purge them of their immature ways.[47] This was also common among Native American Indian tribes in the form of a vision quest.[48]

The transition stage is the period when initiates, who have already begun their journey out of the profane world of childhood, move toward the sacred. This idea of sacred versus profane is central to van Gennep's findings. His idea of the sacred rests upon his theory of regeneration, which states that the energy found in any system gradually winds down and must be recharged.[49] Individuals do this through sleep. Societies do it by initiating successive generations into their adult worlds, which are considered sacred.

Initiates can never go back to their world of games and fantasy. They are banished forever from Never-Never Land and must spend the rest of their lives struggling with adult realities. This represents the movement from religious naivete to a more profound spiritual vision. Lost innocence is not incidental to the process but a direct result of it. It is the goal. But it also makes coming of age difficult for many adolescents who feel caught between two worlds. Although meant to cushion the identity crisis, the transition stage can leave youth disenchanted with the adult world which, finally unmasked, they view as a great disappointment.

Van Gennep's third stage, incorporation, deals with striking a balance between these two realities. This balance is achieved by welcoming the newly-initiated back into the community. Since the newly-initiated have crossed the threshold from the profane to the sacred, upon their return they are given a new status.[50] No longer are they considered immature or childish. Rather, they are afforded all the rights and privileges of other adult members of the community. Males, for instance, can now hunt, make weapons, dance with the adults and take a wife. This is exactly the opposite of what they endured during the transition period, when they were declared *non-status* by their elders. In order for them to go one step up on the status ladder, the uninitiated must first be taken two steps down.[51]

PILGRIMAGE AS RITE OF PASSAGE

An interesting development in the rites of passage that van Gennep observed is the portal. A portal can be any object the uninitiated must pass through, under or into in order to come out the other side, which is sacred.[52] According to van Gennep, this passing may be done between halves of an animal, tree branches or boughs and through any fabricated structure, including tunnels.[53] Van Gennep believed that passage through a portal was an immediate way for the uninitiated to leave the world of the profane and enter the sacred.[54]

As an essential part of the rite, the portal was kept at a distance from the main lodgings and the rest of the community. Eventually, it gave way to the concept of sacred space. In his study of Native American tribes, anthropologist Sam Gill has found belief in sacred space to be nearly universal. He notes that throughout North America there are a number of shrines and physical features significant to many native cultures.[55] These sites are "invested with cosmic significance" and function, among other things, as "world centers, world perimeters, the residences of spirits and gods…and doorways to the spiritual world."[56]

As early as the second century, sacred space in the Judeo-Christian tradition came to mean one of two things: biblical sites in the Holy Land and the tombs of saints and martyrs.[57] The idea of pilgrimage began with the need of the faithful to visit these two types of sites and thereby share in their grace and power. Thus, pilgrimage retained the idea of offering the uninitiated a door to the sacred but also offered something new: distant travel. Instead of walking to the edge of the village or a sacred mountain, as native peoples had done, Christians from Europe traveled to the Holy Land to view the sacred sites firsthand. These early travelers designed their pilgrimages to be challenging and transforming both physically and spiritually. As a rite of passage, pilgrimage served as the portal to the sacred world.

As a modern initiation rite, *Pilgrimage as Rite of Passage* emphasizes not just the goal but the journey itself. This is especially important as parishes and dioceses are adopting the metaphor of faith journey in evangelization and catechesis.[58] The important element of pilgrimage for modern youth is the test or challenge it offers them. It allows them to find out more about themselves and their role in society by showing them who they are in relation to others and what, exactly, they are capable of. It can also give them a sense of separation and independence from authority figures, especially their parents. This separation or independence does not have to be negative, however. It may be seen as passing on the family's or community's rituals/name/identity.

According to one seventeen-year-old who chose a name while on a vision quest:

> Today I made my circle and named myself Lone Stone Among the Rest…Then later this afternoon I sang my name and walked around my circle. Doing this gave my name more depth and meaning. After I had been walking around my circle I had to quit because I was losing my balance. I started singing it again, when I got to my place overlooking the valley. I started to cry, yet I continued. My name symbolizes my cutting the line connecting me to my parents, making me a separate and unique human being.[59]

In writing about the yearly pilgrimage Papago males make from their home in the desert of Southern Arizona to the Gulf of California, Gill has observed characteristics of pilgrimage that transcend gender and culture. He writes:

> We can see that pilgrimage is a very complicated ritual process. At one level, it serves as a rite of passage from youth to manhood. This passage is based both on the performance of a feat requiring the strength of a man and the acquisition of supernatural power through contact with the ocean; and on the visions gained during the pilgrimage. It culminates a childhood of physical and spiritual preparation. It initiates manhood and family life. [60]

This belief in the acquisition of supernatural power during a pilgrimage runs throughout the Christian tradition, and youth ministers in any setting (parish, camp, school, diocese) can make use of it for identity formation and catechesis.

THE CATECHETICAL PROCESS

The best catechesis with youth is often inductive, beginning with their everyday experience and moving toward principles of identity and faith. This process treats the events in a person's life—the building blocks of identity—as the foundation of the faith life of the community.[61] Catechesis begins with the life experience of youth and only after helping them discover their gifts and talents does it pass on the faith story. Therefore, if catechesis is to be effective, it must deal with the stuff of everyday life. This is even more important in an age when ritual and things spiritual are regarded with skepticism and mistrust. We cannot presume faith on the part of youth but must begin with their basic need for belonging.

Religious educator Anne Marie Mongoven of Santa Clara University has developed a process of catechesis that is both experiential and ritualistic.[62] Her process consists of six steps done in a group setting over a two-hour period and forms the basis of the catechesis throughout *Pilgrimage as Rite of Passage.* These steps are: (1) Welcoming, (2) Gathering, (3) Consideration of the Human Experience, (4) Shared Faith Reflection, (5) Acting Justly and (6) Ritual Prayer.[63] Consideration of the Human Experience is perhaps the most important since it touches areas of personal experience that are meaningful to participants. And, as theologian Karl Rahner observed, "Faith is never awakened by someone having something communicated to him purely from outside, addressed solely to his naked understanding."[64] Rather, it is awakening "what has already been *experienced* in the depth of human reality."[65]

Consideration of the Human Experience is the part of catechesis that helps youth discover who they are. This is extremely important at a time in history when rituals and rites of passage are seldom available to help them forge an identity. The perennial question—Who am I?—often goes unanswered or, worse yet, gets answered in destructive ways. What used to be a fast on the sacred mountain has deteriorated into a switching of the tassel on a mortarboard.[66]

Jungian analyst Edith Sullwold attributes this decline to a societal consciousness geared toward individuality. And although true individuality is necessary for catechesis, the ultimate aim of the catechetical process is reintegration into the community, which is surprisingly similar to the last stage of van Gennep's description of the rites of initiation.

Sullwold states:

> The trend of the Western culture has been toward the development of the individual—an individual who is seen as having full freedom of choice to fulfill his own destiny, whether that is within the bounds of his collective or not. One consequence of this development has been the continued breakdown of collective forms. Such seems the case surrounding adolescent ritual in our time. There is almost no social form other than the giving of a license to drive a car, or the privilege of voting and drinking, to mark the passage to adulthood by civil society.[67]

Another Jungian analyst, Jerome S. Bernstein, blames the electronic media for much of this decline, since television, movies and MTV do not engage or challenge youth. They merely provide passive entertainment for a mesmerized audience. In his study of adolescent boys, for instance, Bernstein concluded that:

> Through advertisements which project a static image of the "healthy" male in our society, the media have exerted a powerful influence on the determination of modern standards for the masculine group. Ads tell the adolescent and young adults in our society that he is a true hero if he drinks Coke or smokes Marlboro cigarettes or if he treats girls as though they were mindless maidens in distress. The message is that he need only identify (by imitating their personal habits) with the heroes of the mass media to become a hero. He doesn't have to do the work himself by performing his own heroic deeds or experiencing his own rites

of passage. These ads systematically undermine the process of self-reflection crucial to masculine ego development...The contemporary male is left essentially with three alternatives: 1. to connect up consciously with those legitimate outer rites of passage which survive (or to create new ones), 2. to become aware of the inner rites of passage which take place symbolically within his own psyche and to consciously enact them, or 3. to pay the price for his unconsciousness and disconnectedness from the archetype of initiation with stunted ego development...[68]

Of Bernstein's three alternatives, only the first one regarding legitimate rites of passage offers hope for youth today. Certainly, there are many youth who have moved beyond moratorium and foreclosure, slipping into the unconsciousness and disconnectedness of alternative three. But stunted ego development is not a desired outcome and only serves to confuse identity. Regarding alternative two, Bernstein believes that the major factor in achieving psychological transformation with inner rites of passage "...is the individual's consciousness of the process itself. Without some level of ego participation, either through enactment and/or self-reflection, ritual becomes ritualism."[69]

Bernstein's emphasis on self-reflection bears directly on Mongoven's catechetical process. In order for youth to get the most out of the process, they must first examine themselves emotionally, psychologically and intellectually, both on their own and with the help of the faith community. Without this opportunity for self-reflection, they will be unable to discern their true gifts, which is crucial not only to identity formation, but to fidelity to the Christian message. Nor will they be able to make sense out of the church's faith story, which is the next step in the process.

Of course, this self-reflection is as important for females as it is for males. Unfortunately:

> If the ritual dramas of passage rites are not enacted with personal introspection and discrimination, the individual does not emerge. The magazines that extol the new woman are replete with multiple choice questions with answers gauged from 1 to 5. By adding up her sum total, the new woman can estimate how well she is preparing herself to fit the new stereotype. But the questions are never formulated to help her recognize her own values, her personal strengths and limitations, her own uniqueness. Rather she is encouraged to spend her hard-earned cash on the rituals of expensive magazines, new punk haircuts, Ralph Lauren clothes, and Gucci shoes. She is a "new woman" because she is what a "new woman" is supposed to be. She has no sense of her own individuality. She is wearing a mask. She has avoided the dramatic rites of passage that take long lonely hours of ruthlessly looking at herself and saying, "Yes, this is of value to me, that is of no value." These are the rites of passage that demand the courage to stand alone and say, "This is who I am."[70]

In Mongoven's process, once youth have a chance to build community and examine their own experience, they look at what the church teaches about their experience. This is step four in the process (Shared Faith Reflection), during which participants look at scripture, liturgy, church dogma and teachings and the community's life of service. Youth have an opportunity to connect the reality of their everyday lives to what they previously had considered boring and irrelevant. They also learn that they are part of an on-going, living faith tradition. They have a place in the history of the Christian people and a role to play in today's church.

The last two steps of Mongoven's process, Acting Justly and Ritual Prayer, challenge youth to respond to their problems and struggles as a community. They act as a community by trying to do something either to influence or change the human experience. For instance, in catechetical session one the Prodigal Son acts justly by returning to his father and asking forgiveness of both his father and God. In Erikson's developmental terms, this would be the part of the process that feeds youth's hunger for movement and commitment. Ritual Prayer, then, becomes the *dramatization* of the group's and the church's experience.

PILGRIMAGE AS CATECHESIS

Pilgrimage works catechetically by providing opportunities for youth to experience conversion in a context that makes sense to them (in their own language, stories, music, relationships). It does this while providing movement, identity and ritual expression. Pilgrims build community among themselves while on the journey and, if the journey is extended, while spending days and nights together. During this time they share stories and learn about their faith through the study of scripture, church history or the pilgrimage site itself. Gradually, the church becomes integrated into the developing relationships and witnessing that occur among pilgrims en route to the site. These faith stories weave their way into the emerging identity of youth. Group photos, journals and travel logs help the process.

Even though pilgrimage is catechetical, it moves beyond catechesis by challenging youth physically. Hiking, praying, breaking bread together, reflecting in silence, listening to nature and enduring the hardships of the road present an ideal challenge to youth looking to test themselves. In this sense, pilgrimage has a distinct advantage over other forms of catechesis. Where else can youth experience God's presence and escape the "nagging guilts" of everyday life? Pilgrimage serves as a break from the world of noise and distraction. It is something youth can call their own. It is "an expression of the communitas dimension of any society, the spontaneity of interrelatedness, the spirit bloweth where it listeth."[71]

The most important aspect of pilgrimage for modern youth has to do with identity. As the integrated person emerges from a collage of multiple personae, individual identity forms. Of course, this process lasts throughout adolescence and even into adulthood. Catechetically, this is a critical time for establishing Catholic identity in youth, which is the second advantage pilgrimage has over more common forms of catechesis. Through physical separation, communitas, ordeal and ritual expression, pilgrimage offers an image for youth of what it means to be a young Christian. It does this in a way that blends outer ritual with inner transformation. Anyone who has journeyed to the pilgrimage centers of Jerusalem, Rome, Mexico City, Fatima, Lourdes, Knock or Medjugorje can attest to the deep emotions these experiences inspire.

According to anthropologist Victor Turner:

A pilgrim's commitment, in full physicality, to an arduous yet inspiring journey, is, for him, even more impressive, in the symbolic domain, than the visual and auditory symbols which dominate the liturgies and ceremonies of calendrically structured religion. He only *looks* at these; he *participates* in the pilgrimage way. The pilgrim becomes himself a total symbol, indeed, a symbol of totality; ordinarily he is encouraged to meditate…with the aim of achieving a step toward holiness and wholeness in oneself, both body and soul. But since one aspect of oneself consists of the cherished values of one's own specific culture, it is not unnatural that the new "formation" desired by pilgrims should include a more intense realization of the meaning of that culture. For many that inner meaning is identical with its religious core values.[72]

During World Youth Day 1993 in Denver, Colorado, and World Youth Day 1995 in Manila, the Philippines, youth from around the world celebrated their faith with the Holy Father. Of course, neither of these sites is a pilgrimage center, nor are they considered sacred space. Yet, pilgrims viewed them as sacred by virtue of their gathering. Both Denver and Manila became sacred sites because of the presence of young men and women celebrating their Christian faith together. Sacredness came to be defined not in spatial terms as it had been for van Gennep, Turner and numerous Native American tribes, but *temporally*. In other words, sacredness shifted from *where* to *when*. And the *when* was nothing less than a catechetical moment.

The official record of World Youth Day 1993 in Denver, Colorado, describes the pilgrimage this way:

> The pope said that the work of proclaiming the Gospel could not be done without effort. In fact, he told the youth not to "be afraid to break out of comfortable and routine modes of living, in order to take up the challenge of making Christ known in the modern metropolis."
>
> Many of the pilgrims had already had a taste of what it meant to break away from comfortable living after driving for days, walking for miles, sleeping on the cold ground (if they slept at all), waiting in line for food or to use the portable toilets and not finding any shady relief from the sun.
>
> "It's worth it!" said a group of teenage girls from the Midwestern United States, filling up their water bottles during Mass in front of the McDonald's stand for the third time that morning. "It's awesome. So many people came," chimed in Becky Gentrup of Hartington, Nebraska. "It supports us and helps our faith."
>
> Across the board, it seemed the minor inconveniences these youth experienced did not take away from the significance of meeting the pope and hundreds of thousands of others, nor did it blur the vision of what they were called to do when they returned home.[73]

Youth who participated in this event were catechized in a very positive way. Suddenly it was okay, even "cool," to be Catholic. Hundreds of thousands of youth created an environment that allowed individuals to express their faith and not feel ashamed of it. For many youth, especially younger adolescents, this was something they had never experienced before and led to a new understanding of church as more than the parish community or youth group. Maybe this reflects the new nature of sacredness in these world pilgrimages where, for four or five days, reality is turned upside down and what was once taboo becomes the norm; what was once boring, exciting.[74] For a brief moment in time, communal bonds intertwine with personal identity, and youth achieve a true sense of belonging.[75]

Pilgrimage has the potential to foster conversion in an unprecedented way because it allows youth to enter the faith journey on their own terms (physically, emotionally, communally, ideologically). Modern youth are accustomed to large-scale events lasting for days involving music, group-sharing, ritual and travel. This is a common format in many of their activities. On a pilgrimage, they have the added benefit of being in a loving, supportive community where being Chistian has meaning. Religious educator Berard Marthaler has written that a major function of catechesis involves the "holding together of a shared vision of reality that gives both community as a whole and the persons who constitute it a sense of identity."[76] This is the very essence of pilgrimage, which just might be the ultimate form of catechesis.

Notes

¹See *New Directions in Catholic Youth Ministry: A National Study of Catholic Youth Ministry Program Participants*, cosponsored by the Subcommittee on Youth, National Conference of Catholic Bishops and the National Federation for Catholic Youth Ministry, Bryan T. Froehle, senior research associate (Washington, D.C.: Center for Applied Research in the Apostolate, Georgetown University, 1996), 5, which has determined that "Catholic youth ministry needs to be more persuasive in helping participants understand that reading the Bible is important for growing in their faith…"

²In addition to the resources listed in Chapter 1, see Gertrud Mueller Nelson, "More on Walking Meditation," *Liturgy* 90 27/6 (Chicago: Liturgy Training Publications, 1996), 16. Also, if safety is an issue, then two pilgrims may go together. It may be advisable for the catechist to take the entire group on a day trip to a safe and/or secluded area for the medicine walk.

³See Steven Foster and Meredith Little, "The Vision Quest: Passing from Childhood to Adulthood," in *Betwixt & Between: Patterns of Masculine and Feminine Initiation*, Louise Carus Mahdi, Stephen Foster and Meredith Little, eds. (LaSalle, Ill. Open Court Press, 1987), 93.

⁴C. A. Meier, "Ancient Incubation and Modern Psychotherapy," trans. R. F. C. Hull in *Betwixt & Between*, 422. Again, the catechist needs to adapt the schedule to meet the needs of the youth, team and parish/school.

⁵Adapted from *Celebration of Belonging* (Sacramento, Calif.: Diocese of Sacramento, 1993), 6–7.

⁶See Claire R. Farrer, "Singing for Life: The Mescalero Apache Girls' Puberty Ceremony," in *Betwixt & Between*, 239–63, for a description of chanting and dance in a rite of passage for girls.

⁷The catechist should refer to Bruno Bettelheim's analysis of the fairy tale for background prior to the session. See Bruno Bettelheim, *The Uses of Enchantment: The Meaning and Importance of Fairy Tales* (New York: Vintage Books, 1976), 97–102.

⁸Ibid., 97.

⁹Ibid., 226–27. Bettelheim states: "Male and female figures appear in the same roles in fairy tales; in 'The Sleeping Beauty' it is the prince who observes the sleeping girl, but in 'Cupid and Psyche' and the many tales derived from it, it is Psyche who apprehends

Cupid asleep and, like the prince, marvels at the beauty she beholds. This is just one example. Since there are thousands of fairy tales, one may safely guess that there are probably equal numbers where the courage and determination of females rescue males, and vice versa. This is as it should be, since fairy tales reveal important truths about life."

[10]See Miriam Therese Winter, *Resources for Ritual: Woman Prayer, Woman Song* (Oak Park, Ill: Meyer, Stone, 1987), 75.

[11]Stephen Thomas, "Generation X Writes to the Baby Boomers," *San Francisco Chronicle*, 23 April 1994. This appeared as a letter to the editor.

[12]Ibid.

[13]Erik Erikson, *The Life Cycle Completed* (New York: W. W. Norton, 1982), 32–33.

[14]Erik Erikson, *Identity: Youth and Crisis* (New York: W. W. Norton, 1968), 39. Although stage five deals primarily with teenagers, many young adults in their twenties struggle with issues of identity formation.

[15]Ibid., 23.

[16]Ibid., 242.

[17]Ibid., 244.

[18]Aidan Kavanagh, "The Role of Ritual in Personal Development," in *The Roots of Ritual*, ed. James D. Shaughnessy with an introduction by Aidan Kavanagh (Grand Rapids, Mich.: William B. Eerdmans Publishing, 1973), 149. This is reminiscent of Oscar Wilde's comment that "If an American were given a choice between going to heaven and hearing a lecture on heaven, he would take the lecture." Compare this to Pope Paul VI's *Evangelii Nuntiandi*, which states: "Modern man listens more willingly to witnesses than to teachers, and if he does listen to teachers, it is because they are witnesses" (41) and "modern man is sated by talk; he is obviously often tired of listening and, what is worse, is impervious to words" (42).

[19]J. Eugene Wright, Jr., *Erikson: Identity and Religion* (New York: The Seabury Press, 1982), 85.

[20]David Elkind, *All Grown Up and No Place To Go* (New York: Addison-Wesley, 1984).

[21]Elena Nightingale and Lisa Wolverton, "Adolescent Rolelessness in Modern Society," in *Adolescence in the 1990s: Risk and Opportunity*, ed. Ruby Takanishi (New York and London: Teachers College Press, 1993), 15. "In the past ten to twenty years, rapid erosion of traditional family and social-support networks has added to the difficulties [of finding one's role in society]. Despite the biological, social, and technological changes impinging on adolescent development, especially in this century, there appear to be fundamental human needs that are enduring and crucial to healthy development and survival. These fundamental needs include the need to find a place in a valued group that provides a sense of belonging and the need to feel a sense of worth as a person."

[22]J. Eugene Wright, Jr., *Erikson: Identity and Religion*, 73.

[23]Carol Gilligan, *In A Different Voice: Psychological Theory and Women's Development* (Cambridge, Mass.: Harvard University Press, 1982), 83–84.

[24]Carol Gilligan, "Adolescent Development Reconsidered," in *Mapping the Moral Domain: A Contribution of Women's Thinking to Psychological Theory and Education*, ed. Carol Gilligan, Jane Victoria Ward and Jill McLean Taylor with Betty Bardige (Cambridge, Mass.: Center for the Study of Gender, Education and Human Development, Harvard University Graduate School of Education, 1988), xi–xii.

[25]Carol Gilligan, *In A Different Voice*, 5–23.

[26]Ibid.

[27]Ibid., 46–47.

[28]Ibid., 100. (Italics mine.)

[29]Integration is also the goal in Erikson's life cycle. The integrated individual comes to accept himself or herself, recognizing both goodness and blemishes, successes and failures. Bruno Bettelheim also discusses integration in "The Three Languages: Building Integration" (*The Uses of Enchantment*, 97–102).

[30]Hans-Günther Heimbrock, "Religious Development and the Ritual Dimension," in *Stages of Faith and Religious Development: Implications for Church, Education, and Society,* ed. James W. Fowler, Karl Ernst Nipkow and Freidrich Schweitzer (New York: Crossroad, 1991), 195.

[31]Erikson, *Identity: Youth and Crisis*, 83.

[32]Wendell Berry, *The Unsettling of America* (San Francisco: Sierra Club Books, 1977).

[33]Mary Douglas, *Natural Symbols: Explorations in Cosmology* (New York: Random House, 1970, 1973), 1. Douglas characterized this development as "One of the gravest problems of our day…"

[34]Philip Wheelwright, *The Burning Fountain: A Study in the Language of Symbolism* (Bloomington, Ind.: Indiana University Press, 1954), 171.

[35]Leonel Mitchell, *The Meaning of Ritual*, xi.

[36]Ibid., 117.

[37]See Peter L. Berger, "Modernity as the Universalization of Heresy," in *The Heretical Imperative: Contemporary Possibilities of Religious Affirmation* (Garden City, N.Y.: Anchor Press/Doubleday, 1979), 1–124.

[38]Peter L. Berger, *A Rumor of Angels* (Garden City, N.Y.: Doubleday, 1969), 1–10.

[39]In a typical response to the government's campaign to promote condom use among teenagers, one 15-year-old said: "We're sick of hearing about them." This remark appeared in "To Quote," *Youthworker Update*, March 1994, p. 8.

[40]Mircea Eliade, *Rites and Symbols of Initiation: The Mysteries of Birth and Rebirth* (New York: Harper & Brothers, 1958; reprint, New York: Harper Torchbook, 1965), 3.

[41]Ibid.

[42]Mitchell, *Meaning*, 13. The implication here is that anyone not initiated into the tribe

58

is *not* a human being (e.g., children, strangers, members of other tribes or communities).

[43]Sam D. Gill, *Native American Religions: An Introduction* (Belmont, Calif.: Wadsworth Publishing Company, 1982), 105.

[44]Arnold van Gennep, *The Rites of Passage*, trans. Monika B. Vizedom and Gabrielle L. Caffee (Chicago: University of Chicago Press, 1960), 88–92. Van Gennep originally published *Rites* in 1909.

[45]Ibid., 191–93. Studying initiation rites from around the world, van Gennep observed: "Beneath a multiplicity of forms, either consciously expressed or merely implied, a typical pattern always recurs: the pattern of the rites of passage."

[46]Erik Erikson, "Youth: Fidelity and Diversity," in *Youth: Change and Challenge*, 41. Regarding the relationship between ritual (such as rites of passage) and identity, Erikson argued that "youth has been robbed of the full experience of the *dramatic* transition from adolescence to adulthood and of the *dramatization* of the difference between present and future." (Italics mine.)

[47]Van Gennep, *Rites*, 65–115.

[48]Gill, *Native American Religions*, 97–101. Regarding the vision quest, Gill writes: "At the proper time…a lofty red pine tree was selected. In this tree a platform of woven sticks covered with moss was placed upon a high branch as a bed upon which the youth was to conduct the fast…Left alone in this place, the youth was strictly warned not to take any kind of nourishment or drink. He was to lie quietly day and night on this platform in a patient vigil for his vision."

[49]Van Gennep, *Rites*, viii.

[50]Victor Turner, *The Ritual Process: Structure and Anti-Structure* (Chicago: Aldine Publishing, 1969), 94.

[51]Ibid., 94–106.

[52]Van Gennep, *Rites*, 19–21.

[53]Ibid. Also, for tunnels, see Victor Turner, *Ritual Process*, 27–37.

[54]Van Gennep, *Rites*, 19.

[55]Sam D. Gill, *Native American Religions: An Introduction* (Belmont, Calif.: Wadsworth Publishing Company, 1982), 101.

[56]Ibid.

[57]John Wilkinson, "Jewish Holy Places and the Origins of Christian Pilgrimage," in *The Blessings of Pilgrimage*, ed. Robert Ousterhout (Chicago: University of Illinois Press, 1990), 42–50.

[58]Religious educator Marina Herrera has described the importance of journey in the faith life of Latino youth in "Religion and Culture in the Hispanic Community as a Context for Religious Education: Impact of Popular Religiosity on US Hispanics," *The Living Light* 21/2 (1985): 136–46.

[59]Steven Foster with Meredith Little, *Vision Quest: Personal Transformation in the Wilderness* (New York: Simon & Schuster, 1992), 76.

[60]Gill, *Native American Religions*, 103.

[61]C. Ellis Nelson, *Where Faith Begins* (Atlanta: John Knox Press, 1967), 87–93. Nelson states, "But whether a person is learning life or learning to know God or, as is usually the case, doing both simultaneously, he does so through *events*." (*Emphasis* mine.)

[62]Anne Marie Mongoven, *Living Waters: Signs of the Times* (Allen, Tex.: Tabor Publishing, 1992), iv–x.

[63]Anne Marie Mongoven, "The Catechetical Process," excerpted from material prepared for a course entitled *The Process of Catechetical Ministry* (Santa Clara University, 1988).

[64]Berard L. Marthaler, "Socialization as a Model for Catechetics," in *Foundations of Religious Education*, 76.

[65]Ibid. Marthaler quotes from *Sacramanetum Mundi*, 2:311. (*Emphasis* mine.)

[66]Steven Foster and Meredith Little, "The Vision Quest: Passing from Childhood to Adulthood," in Louise Carus Mahdi, Steven Foster and Meredith Little, eds., *Betwixt & Between: Patterns of Masculine and Feminine Initiation* (La Salle, Ill.: Open Court Press, 1987), 87.

[67]Edith Sullwold, "The Ritual-Maker Within at Adolescence," in *Betwixt & Between*, 116.

[68]Jerome S. Bernstein, "The Decline of Masculine Rites of Passage in Our Culture: The Impact on Masculine Individuation," in *Betwixt & Between*, 144.

[69]Ibid., 138.

[70]Marion Woodman, "From Concrete to Consciousness: The Emergence of the Feminine," *Betwixt & Between*, 210.

[71]Turner, *Image and Pilgrimage*, 32.

[72]Victor Turner, *Dramas, Fields, and Metaphors: Symbolic Action in Human Society* (London: Cornell University Press, 1974), 208.

[73]Catholic News Service and Ignatius Press, *John Paul II Speaks to Youth at World Youth Day* (Washington, D.C.: Catholic News Service, 1993), 91, 107–8.

[74]Turner, *The Ritual Process*, 168–72.

[75]Marthaler, "Socialization as a Model for Catechetics," 79. According to Marthaler, "The model here is Ferdinand Tonnie's *Gemeinschaft*."

[76]Ibid.

Catechist Resources

Bolton, Robert. *People Skills: How to Assert Yourself, Listen to Others and Resolve Conflicts*. New York: Simon & Schuster, 1979. This is an extremely practical resource for learning and using communication skills. It covers barriers to communication, the art of listening, conflict prevention/control and creative problem-solving with groups. It will come in handy for small-group facilitation and counseling individuals.

Catechetical Preparation for the Celebration of Quinceañera. San Jose, Calif.: Diocese of San Jose, 1996. This will prove very helpful with Spanish-speaking versions of the pilgrimage rite. It contains an effective catechetical process for youth and their families that includes scripture, reflection, small-group sharing and ritual prayer. Any part of this process may be incorporated into the rite. English and Spanish versions available.

Catechism of the Catholic Church. Vatican City: Libreria Editrice Vaticana, 1994. This is a must resource, at least for the catechist. If the catechist/team decides to substitute church teaching or dogma for any of the scripture sections in the rite, the *Catechism* offers substantial, authoritative content and guidelines. Care must be taken, however, that the *Catechism* not be used as a textbook for youth.

Clift, Jean Dalby and Wallace B. *The Archetype of Pilgrimage: Outer Action with Inner Meaning*. Mahwah, N.J.: Paulist Press, 1996. This, combined with Victor and Edith Turner's *Image and Pilgrimage in Christian Culture*, gives a solid foundation in the psychological aspects of pilgrimage as a quest for meaning and identity. It provides interesting reading and insights into how pilgrimage works as a journey of faith. Fits nicely with Erik Erikson's life cycle. This would be a good resource for anyone unfamiliar with pilgrimage.

Elkind, David. *All Grown Up and No Place To Go*. New York: Addison-Wesley, 1984. This is a classic youth ministry text that identifies the problem of contemporary youth as growing up too fast and not having a role in society. It addresses the plight of youth struggling with meaning, identity and belonging. Still an excellent resource for understanding adolescent development and the need for children to live a full childhood.

Erikson, Erik H. *Youth: Change and Challenge*. New York: W. W. Norton, 1963, and *Identity: Youth and Crisis*. New York: W. W. Norton, 1968. These are the basic resources for naming identity-formation as the major task of adolescent psychological development. They provide interesting reading for the team member who wants to delve deeper into issues of development.

Foster, Steven with Meredith Little. *Vision Quest: Personal Transformation in the Wilderness*. New York: Simon & Schuster, 1992. This may help the team understand the overnight pilgrimage and naming. It may also clear up questions about visions, fasting, site selection, logistics of camping out, etc.

GIA Publications, 7404 South Mason Avenue, Chicago, Ill. 60638. 1-800-442-1358, FAX 708-496-3828, www.giamusic.com Publisher of "Gather" music book, "RitualSong," liturgical music and tapes. Good overall music resource in English for all parts of the rite.

Gilligan, Carol. *In A Different Voice: Psychological Theory and Women's Development.* Cambridge, Mass.: Harvard University Press, 1982. Good background for the female catechist/team. It challenges traditional views of adolescent development and inspires an appreciation for gender differences. The catechist may want to use this resource for a brief in-service with the team prior to the rite (see also Miriam Therese Winter).

Henriot, Peter J., Edward P. DeBerri and Michael J. Schultheis, eds. *Catholic Social Teaching: Our Best Kept Secret.* Maryknoll, N.Y.: Orbis Books, 1987. Practical resource for **Acting Justly** or **Shared Faith Reflection,** if scripture is not used. Gives outline of major church documents on social teaching as well as historical background on the evolving role of the church. Social justice is an excellent theme for adolescents.

Jackson, Pamela. *Journeybread for the Shadowlands: The Readings for the Rite of the Catechumenate, RCIA.* Collegeville, Minnesota: The Liturgical Press, 1993. Rich and creative resource for learning about salvation history, the catechumenate and ritual in the context of initiation.

Liturgy: Feasts and Fasting, 2/1 (1981). Published by The Liturgical Conference, this is a worthwhile resource on fasting from biblical, sociological and cultural perspectives. Emphasis on fasting as a part of social justice.

Mahdi, Louise Carus, Steven Foster and Meredith Little, eds. *Betwixt & Between: Patterns of Masculine and Feminine Initiation.* With an introduction by Louise Carus Mahdi. La Salle, Ill.: Open Court, 1987. This text offers excellent insight into adolescent development, the need for rites of passage and ritual. It will give the catechist/team an excellent grounding in rites of passage and inspire ideas for adaptation of the rite to local circumstances, including gender.

National Federation for Catholic Youth Ministry (NFCYM). *From Age to Age: The Challenge of Worship with Adolescents.* Washington, D.C.: NFCYM, 1997; *The Challenge of Catholic Youth Evangelization: Called to Be Witnesses and Storytellers* (1993), and *The Challenge of Adolescent Catechesis* (1986). Three excellent, very practical resources for vibrant worship with youth, demonstrating the power of witnessing within catechesis and adolescent faith issues/themes. These will be very helpful for planning liturgies and catechetical sessions as well as for training team members as mentors/guides/models of Christian faith.

Oregon Catholic Press. 1-800-LITURGY, FAX 1-800-4-OCP-FAX, www.ocp.org Publishers of *Liturgia y Canción* and *Flor y Canto* as well as a variety of English and Spanish music titles, liturgy planning aids and liturgical resources.

Prophets of Hope. Vol. 1 "Dawn on the Horizon: Creating Small Communities," Winona, Minnesota: Saint Mary's Press, 1996. This excellent resource offers a detailed process for creating small communities among youth, including meetings, retreats, liturgies, dialogues, discernment, prayer, rituals and a novela. Available in English and Spanish.

Roberto, John, ed. *Faith Maturing: A Personal and Communal Task.* Proceedings of the Second National Symposium on Catholic Youth Ministry. Washington, D.C.: National Federation for Catholic Youth Ministry, 1985. Excellent background on issues of Catholic identity for youth, adolescent sexuality, small-group processing and catechetical method.

Second Vatican Council. *The Rites of the Catholic Church*, vol. 1. New York: Pueblo Publishing, 1990. Good source of alternative scripture for **Shared Faith Reflection** and for prayers, ritual acts, scrutinies, blessings and mystagogia. See the RCIA (especially 75; 138–46; 197–203; 206–36; 244–51; 309–30).

Shelton, Charles. *Adolescent Spirituality: Pastoral Ministry for High School and College Youth*. New York: Crossroad, 1989. Solid background in adolescent development theory, spirituality, morality, sexuality and counseling. Good resource for the catechist to use for team training.

Turner, Victor and Edith. *Image and Pilgrimage in Christian Culture: Anthropological Perspectives*. New York: Columbia University Press, 1978. Insightful analysis of the role of pilgrimage in faith development and identity. Extremely helpful in understanding ritual process and symbols (see also Jean and Wallace Clift).

Van Ornum, William and John Mordock. *Crisis Counseling with Children and Adolescents: A Guide for Non-Professional Counselors*. With an introduction by Eugene Kennedy. New York: Continuum, 1983. Another good resource for background and team training. Deals with issues of separation and abandonment, rebellion, abuse and the "crisis" of a lost sense of self.

Winter, Miriam Therese. *WomanWitness: A Feminist Lectionary and Psalter*. Vol. 2. *Women of the Hebrew Scriptures*. Illustrated by Meinrad Craighead. New York: Crossroad, 1992, and *Woman Prayer/Woman Song: Resources for Ritual*. Oak Park, Ill.: Meyer, Stone, 1987. These are excellent resources for ritual prayer, music, dance, movement, scripture study and social justice for all steps of the catechetical process. Great for consciousness-raising and bonding among girls/young women.

Wolf, Naomi. *The Beauty Myth: How Images of Beauty are Used Against Women*. New York: Doubleday, 1991. Fascinating background for female catechists dealing with self-esteem, image and identity problems among youth and who want to understand some of the cultural/sociological aspects of "beauty."

YouthWorks. Naugatuck, Conn.: The Center for Youth Ministry Development (CYMD), 1994. Foundational resource for "total" youth ministry. Includes material on small/large-group process, group facilitation, ice-breakers, prayer, retreats, evangelization/catechesis, volunteer recruitment/training, budgets, program scheduling, etc. This should be a parish resource for the catechist/team to use at various times during the rite.

Organizations

Baltimore Rites of Passage Kollective, PO Box 7081, Baltimore, MD 21216. 410–225–7012. Good resource for working with African-American youth. Offers rites of passage for both young men and young women in an affirming but challenging environment.

Catholic Youth Organization (CYO). In addition to sports leagues, camping and outdoor activities, some CYOs around the country offer Ropes courses, leadership development programs and rites of passage for inner-city youth. Good resource for the pilgrimage, ritual acts and Medicine Walk.

Cayuga Nature Center, 1420 Taughannock Blvd., Ithaca, NY 14850. 607–273–6260. Offers Ropes courses, outdoor explorations, "eco-awareness" workshops, TEAM Challenge and *Passages for Youth*, which helps youth through leadership development, ritual, community building and contact with nature. Good resource for adapting all steps of the rite.

Center for Youth Ministry Development (CYMD), 175 Church Street, Naugatuck, CT 06770. 203–723–1622. Publishes *YouthWorks* and many excellent resources for "total" youth ministry. Good material on faith sharing, group process, facilitation, leadership training and ritual.

Diocese of San Jose, California. Office of Pastoral Ministry, 900 Lafayette Street, Santa Clara, CA 95050–4966. 408–983–0120; FAX 408–983–0295. "Catechetical Preparation for the Celebration of Quinceañera." Excellent resource for working with Spanish-speaking and bilingual youth.

Institute for Hispanic Liturgy. PO Box 29387, Washington, D.C. 20017-0387. 202-319-6450, FAX 202-529-8729. Excellent resource for Hispanic liturgy, popular devotions and ritual activities with Spanish-speaking communities. Provides materials/conferences in English and Spanish.

The Liturgical Conference, 8750 Georgia Avenue, Suite 123, Silver Spring, MD 20910–3621. 1–800–394–0885. Publishes materials on symbols, ritual, word, eucharist, sacrament and liturgy. Excellent for deeper understanding of the need for ritual and liturgy in an ecumenical setting.

Midway Center for Creative Imagination, 2112 F Street NW, Suite 404, Washington, DC 20037. 202–296–2299. Offers a rite of passage through a course entitled "The Journey," with rituals and physical challenges similar to *Pilgrimage as Rite of Passage*.

National Federation for Catholic Youth Ministry (NFCYM), 3700 Oakview Terrace, NE, Washington, DC 20017. 202–636–3825; FAX 202–526–7544; e-mail: <nfcym@capcon.net> Excellent resource for material on worship with youth, evangelization, catechesis and leadership development.

Rites of Passage, PO Box 148, Sonoma, CA 95476. 707–537–1927; e-mail: <mikeb@sonic.net> Established in 1977, Rites of Passage is an excellent resource for all phases of the rite—prayers,

Circle Dance, pilgrimage, hiking, fasting, naming and the Medicine Walk. Also valuable for team training.

Sacramento Rites of Passage Alliance for African-American Youth, Sacramento, CA. 916–452–3343; e-mail: <srop@igc.apc.org>

School of Lost Borders, The Context Institute at PO Box 946, Langley, WA 98260. 360–221–6044; FAX 360–221–6045; e-mail: <webmaster@context.org>; web site: www.context.org. Established by Steven Foster and Meredith Little, this school offers rituals, fasting, vision quest experience and resources for all aspects of rites of passage.

Star of Peace Retreat Center, 330 West King Road, Ithaca, NY 14850. 607–277–4564. Offers rites of passage and fasting quests in the wilderness. Good resource for fasting, visioning, the Medicine Walk and pilgrimage.